The Smoking Cure

How To Quit Smoking Without Feeling Like Sh*t

Caroline Cranshaw

ISBN: 978-1539397236

First Edition: October 2016

10 9 8 7 6 5 4 3 2 1

Published by Mind Body Health

Auckland, New Zealand

Contact: info@thesmokingcure.com

Contents

4

Dedication

FIRSTLY, I DEDICATE THIS BOOK TO YOU THE READER AND TO ANYONE WHO HAS STRUGGLED WITH ADDICTION. Addiction is a cold hearted bitch, and it's hard not to be one when you are struggling with it.

Secondly, to the love of my life Grant, without your support, unwavering belief in me, reaffirming that I'm not crazy, and amazing editing skills for my dyslexic writing, this book would still be in my head. You are my unicorn.

To my parents, who always believed in me, read and edited my writing when I'm sure it bored the sh*t out of you, as well as giving me a crazy childhood that helped make me unable to be shocked as a therapist.

Last but not least, to my five beautiful, wild-spirited children, Scarlett, Madison, Lance, Alerys, and Ezekeal. Without you, this book would have been finished a year earlier.

The Smoking Cure Objectives

1. To guide you in the process of quitting smoking for good.

2. To help you gain insight on why you became addicted and started smoking.

3. To bring you awareness of why smoking has been so hard to quit.

4. To teach you how to be completely committed to being a non-smoker.

5. To help you be clear about what future you want and are creating.

6. To give you powerful tools to release your addiction to nicotine.

7. To help you change yourself into a vibrant, healthy, non-smoker.

Introduction

"Whether you sniff it smoke it eat it or shove it up your ass, the result is the same: addiction." ~ William S. Burroughs

SO, YOU FEEL LIKE YOU ARE READY TO QUIT SMOKING... You can't change something if you don't acknowledge the problem or make a plan of action to fix it. Now, I am assuming that you're not content with being addicted to cigarettes or you probably wouldn't be reading this. You're unhappy with the fact that you smoke and want to change it.

Let's be honest. When it comes to quitting smoking, going cold turkey is not only hell, but most of the time, it doesn't work. We start out with the best intentions, but once the withdrawals set in, we feel so awful we give up and start smoking again. If you are ready to stop smoking for good without feeling like sh*t, you need a different approach.

The first step to change is awareness, and the next is acceptance. I find most people say they want to stop smoking, but they are not clear about when that will happen. They are not sure what their present status really is. In order to change, you need to take a good, hard look at where you are now and then where you want to be. Most of us have our head in the sand about smoking because we don't want to face it.

It feels too painful to actually face what smoking is doing to your health, happiness and appearance. But, (and possibly a horrible smelly cigarette butt), it's more painful not to be as healthy, happy, not to mention as sexy, as you know you could be if you were free of the habit of smoking.

I was a pack-a-day-plus smoker for over ten years. I quit many times but always found it a massive struggle and would find myself back puffing away before long. I tried patches, gum and prescription medication hoping that it would be the magic bullet that finally broke the spell cigarettes seemed to have over me.

I tried every therapy, pill and healing technique I could find in my quest to quit. I became a hypnotherapist, traveled the world and trained with the top therapists, healers, and scientists to learn the most efficient methods to heal addiction disorders.

Coming from a family of addicts, as well as struggling with several other addictions, I truly know what it's like to struggle with addiction and what it takes to overcome it.

I created this program after I tried everything - and I mean everything, to figure out what really works to heal nicotine addiction. I have now helped thousands of people to stop smoking for good and have compiled and created tips, supplements, and techniques that are fast, effective and easy.

In this book, I will take you through a 7 step process to break free of your addiction. We will start with identifying why nicotine has been so hard for you quit, what happens in your brain and body when you are addicted to nicotine. I will then take you through a series of exercises that will help you give up your excuses and be totally committed to quitting smoking for good.

Next, I will help you identify what supplements will help to balance out your neurotransmitters and individual body chemistry to make the process of quitting much easier for you. I will then teach you several techniques that you will be able to use to manage your cravings as they come up as well as reprogram your mind to be a non-smoker at every level.

You will then be able to personalize and follow the quit smoking action plan that will transform you into the non-smoker you want to be. I also give you advice on how to handle the issues that come up as you navigate the process of overcoming your smoking addiction for good.

Hopefully, I will help you find the missing key to overcoming your addiction to smoking for good, by helping you create an individual program which addresses the physical, emotional and spiritual aspects that keep you addicted to smoking, and help you to access the inner calm and happiness you desire and deserve.

Step 1: Awareness

"Quitting smoking is easy. I've done it hundreds of times."

~ Mark Twain

WHY IT'S BEEN SO F#*&ING HARD TO STOP...

We know it's not good for us - so why do we do it?

Nicotine, along with caffeine and alcohol, is one of the three most widely used legal drugs. According to the US surgeon-general, "Smoking will continue as the leading cause of preventable, premature mortality for many years to come."

Approximately 1 billion people around the world smoke. An estimated 22.5% of adults in the world (1 billion people) smoke tobacco products (32.0% of men and 7.0% of women[i]). It's estimated that 6% of deaths in females and 11% of deaths in males each year are caused by tobacco use.[ii]

According to the World Health Organization, approximately 5 million people a year die prematurely as a result of smoking. And if it keeps going the way it is, smoking will kill up to a billion people worldwide this century as stated by John Seffrin, chief executive of the American Cancer Society.

5 million people a year... That's around 14,000 people a day, dying from smoking-related diseases.

Smoking kills more than 50% of all smokers, mainly from cancer, and even though it's the single largest avoidable risk of premature death, there are approximately 30 million new smokers a year, as estimated by scientists.

The average smoker lives ten years less than a non-smoker and is much more likely to contract many different, horrible diseases.

So why, when we know that cigarettes are poisonous and that they make us much more likely to die of a horrible disease do we continue to smoke? Blame it on the nicotine. The main stimulant in cigarettes, nicotine, has a substantial effect even in tiny doses.

Can you remember your first cigarette? It probably tasted awful, burned your throat and lungs (if you inhaled), and made you feel dizzy and nauseous. Those are some of its toxic effects in action. A few more puffs, and for most people, the body no longer rebels. In fact, you rather like it. In short, you're hooked.

Nicotine's mood-altering effects are somewhat unique, as it is both a stimulant and a relaxant. It causes a release of glucose (sugar) from the liver, and adrenaline, making you feel more alert and calm at the same time. When you tried quitting smoking before, did you feel anxious, achy, tired, irritable and hungrier than usual?

Did you crave sweets more than normal, feel slightly dizzy, foggy-headed or even slightly confused? If you did, you were likely experiencing low blood sugar symptoms. That's because every cigarette you smoke triggers a small blood sugar release.

When you quit smoking, your blood sugar can become lower than before since you are no longer having that blood sugar boost from smoking.

When you smoke a cigarette, nicotine passes from the lungs to the brain within seven seconds and immediately triggers the release of a heady chemical cocktail such as acetylcholine, adrenalin, dopamine, endorphins, and serotonin.

The release of these hormones and neurotransmitters is what is mostly responsible for nicotine's psychoactive effects.

Nicotine appears to enhance alertness, concentration, and memory, as well as reducing anxiety and pain at the same time. It's no surprise so many people are hooked on smoking.

However, don't be fooled by the payoffs that nicotine can give. It is more deadly than arsenic and strychnine. The lethal dosage of nicotine for a 150 pound or 68 kg adult is 60 mg.

The lethal dosage for strychnine is 75 mg and the lethal dosage for arsenic is 200 mg. In other words, nicotine is one and one-quarter times as toxic as strychnine and more than three times as toxic as arsenic.

Something doesn't feel right about having to consume a poisonous substance to get through your day, and for you to be able to cope. You've probably also found that the original kick you got from smoking isn't nearly as good as it used to be.

You may have noticed that cigarettes don't actually make you feel good at all. You just don't feel as bad as you feel when you were craving one.

That craving for cigarettes is partly due to your subconscious believing you need nicotine. When it's in your system all the time, your body starts to think that it needs to be there for your survival - just like air, food, and water.

The pull of nicotine comes from the fact that it brings relief. Unfortunately, this relief is only temporary. You might also have found that your relationship with smoking actually causes you problems or gets in the way of your ability to function in the world in one way or another.

Not many smokers realize that a lot of the stress relieved by a cigarette is caused by smoking the one before.

The stress on your body, brought on by being poisoned by the thousands of toxic chemicals, triggers the release of endorphins. Endorphins are our natural pain relieving chemical. Endorphins are more potent than morphine or heroin!

To guarantee it has a "painkilling" supply for the next assault (or cigarette), the body stockpiles endorphins and waits for the next cigarette to release them.

When the expected chemical trigger from smoking doesn't arrive, the smoker experiences increasing stress from low blood sugar and low endorphins and craves the endorphin and sugar hit they now associate with smoking another cigarette.

The cycle works something like this: experience stress, smoke a cigarette, trigger an endorphin and blood sugar release, feel a temporary relaxation, deplete endorphin supply and blood sugar, experience increased stress. And round and round we go...

Recap

- 5 million people a year, approximately 14,000 people a day, die from smoking related diseases.

- Nicotine is one and one-quarter times as toxic as strychnine and more than three times as toxic as arsenic.

- Nicotine is both a stimulant and a relaxant.

- Nicotine causes a release of glucose (sugar) from the liver, and adrenaline, making you feel more alert and calm at the same time.

- When you quit smoking, your blood sugar can become lower than before causing you to feel dizzy, foggy-headed and irritable.

- Your craving for cigarettes is partly due to your subconscious believing you need nicotine when it's in your system all the time; your body starts to think that it needs to be there for your survival - just like air, food, and water.

- The stress on your body, brought on by being poisoned by the thousands of toxic chemicals when you smoke, triggers the release of endorphins. Your body will wait to release endorphins until the next cigarette.

- The smoking cycle: experience stress, smoke a cigarette, trigger an endorphin and blood sugar release, feel a temporary relaxation, deplete endorphin supply and blood sugar, experience increased stress - want another cigarette to feel better.

My Story

*"If you want something you've never had, you must be willing to
do something you've never done."*

~ Thomas Jefferson

I GREW UP IN A FAMILY OF SMOKERS, not mention alcoholics and drug addicts. Some of them highly educated and extremely successful, others I wouldn't be surprised to see on an episode of Cops. I have found when it comes to addiction, the level of intelligence and socio-economic status doesn't seem to be a factor.

If you name an addiction, I pretty much can guarantee I or someone in my family has had it. Being genetically disposed to having an addictive personality and environmentally exposed to smoking, it's no surprise I became hooked on cigarettes by the time I was thirteen.

I remember smoking my first cigarette at nine.

My grandmother would have me look out for her while she snuck a smoke in the backyard. My grandfather, a well-respected doctor, had quit smoking and wanted her to stop as well.

My grandmother was not a woman who could be told what to do, plus her gin and tonics just weren't the same without a cigarette in hand. She used to say to me, in her deep, southern drawl "I can't stand cigarettes. I hate this one so much, I'm going to burn it right now." Winking at me as she lit up.

I would stand there smirking, watching out for my grandfather, as my granny told me never to let a man tell me what to do. It was our secret, and she always talked to me like I was an adult, making me feel special. I remember stealing a cigarette and matches and skipping to my best friend's house, trying to look innocent, but my heart was pounding in my throat.

We ran down to the creek on that hot summer's afternoon, the sound of cicadas vibrating in the air and I felt so sophisticated lighting up that cigarette, pulling the smoke into my lungs.

I recall the terrible taste, my throat and lungs constricting in shock, and coughing to the point I feared my lungs were going to turn inside out. My head began to spin, and I was afraid my lunch was about to come back up. I laid down on the dried leaves next to the creek, listening to the water trickling over the rocks. My friend Leslie lay next to me on the ground. I felt as though I was spinning.

My first high... I felt sick, but at the same time, it felt so naughty, so rebellious, so grown up that I knew that I would be a smoker as an adult.

By the time I was thirteen, I was sneaking into the back of the local pizza parlor and buying packs of cigarettes with my babysitting money from the vending machine. My mother, a hardworking single mother, was a heavy smoker, so she made a good target to steal cigarettes from if I needed to. My mother smoked in the house and never seemed to notice the fact that I reeked of cigarettes.

I can remember smoking in my bedroom, listening to Prince, reading fashion magazines, smoking one ciggie after the other, being repulsed by the taste of the cigarettes but knowing if I just push through the disgust, I would start to enjoy it.

By the time I was sixteen, my mother had given up trying to tell me I shouldn't smoke. I loved to sit and smoke with her and her eclectic group of friends, every race, and sexual orientation, all of them smokers. I loved feeling so grown up.

I wish I could go back and talk to that younger self, to tell her how unglamorous smoking truly was. However, I doubt she would have listened to me. At the same time, I believe I was meant to be a smoker so that I could learn how to quit smoking effectively and teach it to others.

At eighteen, my pack a day habit was truly a part of my persona. I dressed all in black, smoked with a black cigarette holder and kept my cigarettes in a silver case. When people made comments to me like "second-hand smoke kills", I would stare into their eyes, inhale dramatically, and blow smoke in their face. "Not fast enough..." I would reply with a smirk on my face.

I was a smoker. It was a shield, a part of my mask. A way of telling people not to f**k with me or they would be sorry. I thought I was a combination of Marilyn Monroe, Audrey Hepburn, and Sharon Stone rolled into one.

I carried on smoking heavily until I was 27. Then I had a head-on car accident with a truck on New Year's Eve. I had facial reconstruction, a head injury, broke multiple bones and had a kneecap reattached. That still wasn't quite enough to stop me.

As soon as I could drag myself along the handrails of the hospital corridors, I was off to the smoker's area, bumming cigarettes off the other patients. It probably took me 30 minutes to hobble 100 meters, but I was determined.

I remember the first time I made it there, looking around at the other people smoking, some with oxygen tanks or even in hospital beds - puffing away. I realized how sad we all looked, how stupid it was to smoke. However, the relief of that first drag, the nicotine hitting my system overpowered any desire to quit.

I continued to smoke through my rehabilitation - smoking as I limped along on my frequent walks. Totally unable to bend my right knee, I must have looked ridiculous shuffling down the street as I dragged on my cigarette.

It was not a cool look and for the first time I wanted to quit. My accident taught me that my health was the most important asset I had. More important than love, money, and success. That without my health, I struggled to enjoy life.

Smoking was something I was doing that was impacting my health and my body's ability to heal. It was setting me up to have even more health issues and it was time to stop.

In my first attempt, I tried patches. I still craved smoking, and I had the most horrific nightmares ever. I lasted three days. Waking up in a cold sweat from a dream that had dead bodies everywhere (which seemed to go on for hours,) I stumbled outside hyperventilating. I grabbed the butt of a cigarette I found and lit up, a wave of nausea washed over me, and I promptly threw up.

I felt like a heroin addict and knew I needed help. The next day, I got a script from my doctor for Zyban. I felt hopeful and motivated, as I popped my first pill and smoked my tenth cigarette of the day. I was giving up after all, so I might as well enjoy my last day as a smoker.

That hopefulness turned to frustration within a few days, as the Zyban seemed to make me want to smoke more, plus my hands had started to shake like I had Parkinson's.

Next, it was acupuncture, which seemed to make no difference to my desire to smoke but did help my nerve pain from the accident. I tried nicotine gum, to which I had an allergic reaction. The gum caused my lips to swell up, making me look like I had the worst lip fillers ever. Months went by, and I was still smoking a pack or more a day. I was starting to feel hopeless and afraid that I was never going to kick this habit.

One Saturday afternoon, in the middle of one of my frequent pity parties of how I would never be able to kick my dirty filthy habit, my fur-baby "Cosmo," a Jack Russell with ADHD, was begging me for a walk. Still feeling sorry for myself, I shuffled down to the local park and sat on a bench puffing from walking two blocks.

I saw a little girl with gorgeous blonde curls around four years old pick up a cigarette butt and bring it to her mother, holding it to her mouth like she was smoking.

Her mother grabbed it away from her, horrified and said "Oh no darling, cigarettes are poison! Mommy would never let you smoke a cigarette. I love you way too much!" She gave her daughter a big cuddle, "Mommy only wants you to put good things into your body! You have to love and look after your body – it's the only one you have."

For me, it was as if time stood still, and I realized that I was treating my body like sh*t. That I had to love myself and my body just like that mother loves her little girl. I would never let a child I cared about smoke a cigarette. So why didn't I protect and look after myself? That if I truly loved myself, I would never smoke or do anything to treat my body like crap.

After my accident I was lucky to be alive, let alone walking and instead of treating my body with the love and care it deserved, I was filling it with poison. That was it. I was going to do whatever it took to finally defeat the evil force that my nicotine addiction had become. Cigarettes were my enemy, and I was going to figure out how to break the hold they had on me and maybe even help other people too...

A friend called me to tell me she was going to go to a hypnotherapist to quit smoking. I felt strangely excited. I had read a book on hypnosis as a ten-year-old (I was a weird child) and went through a phase of telling everyone I was going to hypnotize people for a living when I grew up. I found out when she was going and called to make an appointment with the hypnotherapist myself.

I remember going to the appointment, not believing it would work. The hypnotherapist was a very nice older lady, and I can remember chatting with her about why I wanted to quit. When it was time to do the relaxation, I lay back in a huge, creaky leather recliner, she turned off the lights, had me close my eyes and started to talk in a soothing voice.

I remember listening to her, but at the same time, listening to the traffic outside and trying to decide what I was going to have for lunch.

Different thoughts kept popping into my head. "Am I hypnotized? This office smells funny. What if someone walked in right now? Would I be able to stand up quickly?" The relaxation seemed to last around ten minutes, however, when she told me to open my eyes, I could see that over a half an hour had passed.

I paid my money, and as I was walking to my car, I called my friend who had an appointment later that afternoon. I told her it was a load of crap, and that she should cancel her appointment and not waste her money.

Three days later, I realized I hadn't had a single cigarette and hadn't even thought about smoking. I started to experience cravings but was determined not to smoke. I kept telling myself that I wasn't going to have a cigarette because I don't smoke.

I started to research other ways of dealing with my cravings, a lot of which are included in this program.

Eventually, I trained as a hypnotherapist and health coach. A lot of the work I do is helping people overcome their struggle with addictions. I have worked with thousands of smokers and have tried many different techniques to figure out what actually works with nicotine addiction.

I understand what it's like to be addicted to smoking, and I know it's possible to overcome it. Not every technique I use is going to work for you, however, some will. I think you are ready to quit, otherwise, you wouldn't be reading this now.

There comes a point when we get sick of our own bullsh*t, stop making excuses and realize we need help. We all need someone to hold our hand, and tell us that they believe in us, even when we don't believe in ourselves.

I'd like to be that person for you, to guide you through the process and calm you down when you feel like it's too hard. I believe that are you are much stronger than you realize, that your ability to change and fulfill your potential is beyond what you could imagine. You just need some new tools and rituals to make it happen.

Have you failed at quitting smoking before? Yes, but at least you were trying. You have to keep trying, and this time, actually commit to it and believe without a doubt that you will be able to stop smoking for good.

It takes perseverance to be good at something. Watching a toddler learn to walk is a lesson in persistence. No matter how many times they fall, they keep getting back up. You don't see them trying to walk a few times and then give up. You have just been practicing at being a non-smoker, and now you are going to master it.

Taming Your Lizard

"When your mind is preoccupied, your impulses - not your long-term goals - will guide your choices." ~ Kelly McGonigal

NOW YOU CONSCIOUSLY KNOW THAT SMOKING IS bad for you. However, there are parts of your brain that thinks smoking is good. It's important to look at these parts of your brain to understand why it would believe smoking is something you should continue to do.

Your brain has many different components. The part of your brain that knows smoking is bad is the most advanced (we'll call it your computer brain). Under that, lies more primitive layers which we will refer to as your animal and reptilian brain.

Humans have 3 independent yet connected parts to our brain, commonly referred to as the Triune Brain: The reptilian section, the limbic section, and the neocortex section. Each section serves a purpose.

The Reptilian section is your first and oldest brain regarding our evolution. It's the instant fight or flight survival part of the brain. It evolved to serve your genes by driving essential needs.

Operating behind the scenes, it drives and regulates our instinctive survival needs: hunger, oxygen, heart rate, blood pressure, sleeping, waking and self-preservation, among many others. Because of this, the reptilian brain is very animalistic and primitive in nature.

It closely resembles the brain of present-day reptiles such as lizards, snakes, crocodiles, and alligators. Your reptilian brain is part of your unconscious or subconscious mind, and its primary role is to make sure that you stay alive.

It does not learn from its mistakes and understands only images, not language. This is a large part of what drives the need to smoke once you are addicted.

The Limbic section or Animal brain is the part of the brain that first developed in mammals. It generates our emotions and feelings regarding our current reality. Most of its functions involve the four f's; feeding, fighting, fleeing, and f**king...

This part of our brain triggers fear, pleasure and rage. It's the part of the brain that rewards you when you engage in something it deems pleasurable.

The Neocortex section is the most advanced part of the brain, the source of higher thought. It generates awareness, consciousness, empathy, logic and rational thinking. This is the part of the brain that knows you should quit smoking but battles this with your animal and reptile brains. Your computer brain wants you to quit smoking.

Your reptilian/animal brain is driven to do whatever feels good. So when you quit smoking, your computer brain is taking over and saying "Right, I have had enough of you poisoning yourself with those filthy cigarettes. No more smoking!"

It may last a while; you may think you have finally quit smoking. However, in the battle between the reptile and the computer brain, the reptile will win in moments when you are weak.

When you have been drinking or using drugs, your computer brain has less control and the reptile brain is much stronger. This is why people tend to make bad decisions when they are intoxicated.

To keep your lizard/animal brain under control when you are experiencing cravings, it's important to try to relax and see it for what it is.

This is that part of our brain that is broadcasting survival fears, trying to keep us safe. Since it's use to having nicotine in your system, it believes it needs it to survive.

When you stop smoking, it sets off an alarm. "Whoop, whoop, we are low on nicotine. Hurry up and get me a smoke, pronto!" Just like how you become "hangry" when you need to eat, your brain will cause you to feel uncomfortable until it gets what it believes is lacking.

Taming the Lizard Brain Exercise

I WANT YOU TO CHOOSE A REPTILE OR ANIMAL THAT WILL REPRESENT THIS PART OF YOUR BRAIN TO HELP YOU PUT IT IN PERSPECTIVE.

1. Pick a reptile or animal that will represent that part of your brain. It could be a lizard, a snake, a monkey, a parrot, anything that works for you. It's helpful to find a toy, a piece of jewelry or stuffed animal that you can carry or place somewhere you will see it often. Or just find a picture of one you can save on your phone to look at.

2. When you have a craving, imagine that reptile or animal is there with you. You can pat it on the head, thank it for sharing and tell it firmly "I NEVER smoke NOW." This part of you doesn't understand consequences, or the past or the future, but it does understand never and now.

3. Tell your animal thank you for your input, but no, you are not going to smoke. Say it nicely. This part of you only wants to help to keep you safe.

Personally, I picture my lizard as a green iguana named Freda, who has a heavy Yiddish accent.

I find this exercise helpful for any craving you are trying not to succumb to. Craving alcohol, porn, drugs, sugar or Facebook? This is also that part of you that tells you that there is not enough: not enough money, not enough potential partners if you are single, not enough food, or even not enough shoes...

Oh, and someone is probably going to come and try to take your things and hurt you. These thoughts were helpful for our survival when we were living in caves, however in the present day, not so much.

My lizard used to always be in my ear, telling me to smoke and eat crap food since no one likes me anyways, oh and my partner is going to leave me, I'm going to run out of money and end up homeless. I imagine patting her head, thanking her and telling her not to worry, I've got it covered. I tell her to go sit on a rock in the sun and relax, everything is okay.

Your lizard is only trying to help. Becoming aware of what it's saying is enlightening and not listening when it's not based in fact is empowering.

Freda is kind of like my great-grandmother, who use to warn me to never go anywhere alone since evil men would snatch me off the street or to never use tampons since that would mean I wasn't a virgin, and no man would ever want to marry me.

She meant well, but, really, her fears were so out there it was hilarious. Learning to laugh at your lizard is the secret to living a life free of being controlled by your fears.

Recap

- Humans have 3 independent yet connected parts to our brain. The reptilian section, the limbic section, and the neocortex section.

- The Reptilian section is your first and oldest brain in regards to our evolution. It's the instant fight or flight survival part of the brain. It drives and regulates our instinctive survival needs.

- It does not learn from its mistakes and understands only images, not language. This is a large part of what drives the need to smoke once you are addicted.

- The Limbic section or Animal brain is the section of the brain that first developed in mammals. Most of its functions involve the four f's; feeding, fighting, fleeing, and f**king... This is the part of the brain that rewards you when you engage in something it deems pleasurable.

- When you have a craving, imagine that reptile or animal is there with you. You can pat it on the head, thank it for sharing and tell it firmly "I NEVER smoke NOW."

Step 2: Insight

How Your Excuses Are Keeping You Stuck

"It is only when we have the courage to face things exactly as they are without any self-deception or illusion that a light will develop out of events by which the path to success may be recognized." ~ I Ching

NOW THAT WE ARE CLEAR ON WHY IT'S SO HARD TO stop, we are going identify the bullsh*t excuses you tell yourself that keep you smoking, pinpoint your personal reasons for quitting and prepare you for the mental process of quitting.

Why Do You Keep Smoking?

Once you've started smoking it can be very hard to stop. You may smoke because it wakes you up in the morning, helps you focus, feels satisfying after a meal, relaxes you when you're stressed, curbs your appetite, is the perfect excuse for a break or gives you something to do when you are bored. Anything that offers you all that is very appealing.

To start, we need to cure you of your lame excusitis* that's been plaguing you. *Definition of EXCUSITIS. A person who is suffering from the sickness of MAKING EXCUSES.

You know, all the bullsh*t excuses you come up with to justify why you continue to smoke. The key to stop making excuses that keep you smoking is to examine how much you view life as being within your control.

I find the first step to change any unhealthy habit is to understand something called locus of control.

Internal locus of control is when we assume responsibility for our actions and believe we are in charge of our lives.

External locus of control is when we protect ourselves by blaming others or circumstances and not take ownership of our failures or mistakes. The more you have an internal locus of control, the more you feel in control of your actions, happiness, and life.

External locus of control - Out of control.
Internal locus of control - In control.

Most of us are living in reaction to the world around us, rather than grabbing the wheel. Or we feel like we are trying to grab the wheel from someone else, but we never seem to get in the driver's seat. And that's frustrating!

To start taking full responsibility and take control of your life, you have to stop making excuses...

Our excuses are made to move blame away from ourselves to others, or things we consider outside of our control. If you tell people that you can't quit smoking because your partner or your family and friends smoke, you are shifting the blame to someone else and not taking personal responsibility.

Recap

- Internal locus of control is when we assume responsibility for our actions and believe we are in charge of our lives.

- External locus of control is when we protect ourselves by blaming others or circumstances and do not take ownership of our failures or mistakes. The more you have an external locus of control, the less you feel in control of your actions, happiness, and life.

- Excuses are mostly made to move blame away from ourselves to others or things we consider outside of our control. If you tell people that you can't quit smoking because your partner or your family and friends smoke, you are shifting the blame to someone else and not taking personal responsibility.

My Excuses For Why I Can't Stop Smoking...

I can't stop smoking because...

So what are your excuses?

IF YOU SAID I SMOKE BECAUSE I'M STRESSED, I think it's important to track back to why you're stressed. Are you stressed because you hate your job? Or are you stressed because you're not happy in your relationship? If you don't get to the core of why you're smoking or more importantly, what you're avoiding dealing with, it's going to be a much bigger struggle to quit.

Our excuses lead us back to what we need to deal with and what we are avoiding. Take a few minutes to write down every excuse you have used or tell yourself either in your workbook or on a separate piece of paper.

Client Story

A good example of this is a client I had a few years ago who came to me for stress management and anxiety. Tall, boyish good-looks, in his late thirties, "Matthew" *(not his real name), pulled up in a Ferrari that cost more than most people's houses. A highly successful hedge fund manager, he looked like he had it all together.

As I started to question him about his lifestyle, I was surprised to hear that while he had been a social smoker for a few years, over the past few months it had escalated to thirty to forty cigarettes a day. When I pointed out that quitting smoking would help reduce his anxiety, he said he couldn't quit smoking because he was too stressed.

When I asked what was causing him to be so stressed that he needed to smoke that much, he snapped. He told me to mind my own business and just hypnotize him to stop being so stressed. I said that if he weren't willing to address why he was so stressed and what he was avoiding by smoking heavily, it probably wouldn't work.

He looked so upset, I thought he was going to burst into tears. He admitted in a trembling voice that he had recently discovered his wife was having an affair with her personal trainer. When he mentioned the personal trainer's name, I realized that I knew him personally, having briefly trained with him years ago myself.

The personal trainer was a Fabio-type character, well known for having affairs with wealthy married women. I had seen several clients who had fallen for his charms, only to be left heartbroken and crying their eyes out in my office after he moved on to the next conquest.

I asked my client if had confronted his wife and he said no. He had suspected something was going on and had hired a private investigator to confirm it. Once he had proof, he went to the man's house and told him to never talk to his wife again, or he would spend every last cent he had destroying him.

This would be a terrifying threat coming from such a powerful and wealthy man. The personal trainer begged for forgiveness and promised he would never see his wife again.

He assumed the man had made good on his promise since his wife had been acting depressed and bitchy ever since he had visited her lover. I asked why he hadn't told his wife he knew, and he replied he didn't want to deal with it. That he would rather forget it ever happened and stay married.

He had three young children, and he didn't want them to go through what he did, as his parents had divorced when he was young due to his father having affairs. His mother had never remarried and remained bitter to this day, and his father was on his fifth unhappy marriage.

No wonder the guy was stressed and chain smoking! I explained that I believed it was important to talk to his wife about what he knew. Otherwise, he would end up as bitter as his mother if he didn't die of lung cancer first.

He replied in an angry tone that he knew what was best for him and his family and would I just get on with it and hypnotize him to stop his anxiety attacks and make him forget the whole damn thing!

I agreed with him, maybe he did know what's best, but if he was wrong - the universe has a way of making things happen. It nudges people in the right direction, and if he was supposed to tell his wife that he knew, the universe would give him a sign.

It was up to him whether or not he listened. He rolled his eyes, and I proceeded to do a guided visualization with him, seeing himself in the future - relaxed, a non-smoker, happy and healthy.

As he walked out, I reiterated that I believed, although it was scary, it would be beneficial, to be honest with his wife. He replied with a sneer, "Or the universe will give me a sign?

Yeah, right. I'll be sure to let you know when the universe sends me that sign..."

"Please do" I grinned. "Everything is going to be okay in the end, I promise," I called after him. He waved in dismissal as he got in his car. I silently wished him well, hoping the best possible outcome for him as I do with all of my clients.

I finished my paperwork, as he was my last client of the day. I was picked up for a date a half an hour later with a new man, with which a friend had set me up. My date suggested a Japanese place close by that was always fully booked. I said we could try, not very hopeful of getting a table, since, in my own experience, you needed to book there a week in advance.

When we arrived at the restaurant, we were told sorry - they were fully booked as usual. As we were walking out, the owner called us back, saying someone had just called to cancel their reservation, and we could have a table right away.

We were then seated right next to my client and his wife! The tables were very close together, I was seated next to my client's wife, my date sitting next to my client. I smiled politely at my client with my best poker face while he looked like he was going to pass out from the shock, his face turning white and then a sickly green.

To top it off, I knew his wife, as our daughters took gymnastics together. She greeted me by name with a friendly smile, "Hi Caroline. How are you?" She turned to her husband, introducing us. "Honey, you should go see Caroline to help you quit smoking. I hear she's very good. Maybe this is a sign..."

He looked so stunned he couldn't even get a word out, he just nodded his head blankly. "I would be happy to help; I personally am a big believer in signs," I replied with a smile, as I handed over my card.

I then proceeded to have a very awkward dinner with my date, while my client and his wife struggled to make conversation. Both of them looking like they would rather be somewhere else, the unsaid words they were both afraid to say hanging in the air.

The next day, I received a call from my client. "So was that a sign?" he croaked. "Honey, I would call that a billboard with neon flashing lights," I replied with a laugh. I ended up doing a few more sessions with him, supporting him through calmly confronting his wife, quitting smoking and subsequently, his divorce.

I ran into him last month with his new fiancée, looking radiantly happy. He told me that, in the end, he and his ex-wife are much happier with their new partners than they were together. Their children are doing great, and he can't believe he ever was a smoker in the first place.

Breakdown Your Excuses Exercise

SO, IS THERE SOMETHING IN YOUR LIFE THAT YOU'RE NOT DEALING WITH? What excuses are keeping you stuck and addicted to smoking?

So let's take those excuses and break each one down.

1. I smoke because I'm miserable in my relationship, job, living arrangement, etc. and smoking helps me forget how unhappy I am.

a) Smoking instead of facing my marriage and doing something to change it only keeps me stuck.

b) If I stop smoking, I can start to deal with why I'm not happy and make changes that will result in me being happier.

c) I am looking forward to quitting smoking, so I can face what I am avoiding and make positive changes in my life.

2. I smoke because I feel antsy if I don't have a cigarette every few hours.

a) I feel antsy because I am having withdrawals from nicotine.

b) If I stop smoking, I will feel uncomfortable for a few days and then I will stop having withdrawals.

c) Therefore, I am looking forward to quitting smoking, so I stop feeling uncomfortable when I don't smoke.

Get the jist?

I smoke because...

Take a few minutes to breakdown down your excuses either in your workbook or on a separate piece of paper to help you see how ridiculous they are.

Why Do You Want To Quit?

ARE YOU STRESSED ABOUT HOW MUCH YOU SPEND on cigarettes? Or put another way, are you stressed about how much money you waste on cigarettes? Are you fed up with having to go outside to smoke by yourself? Or perhaps you are sick of the pressure from your loved ones to quit? Maybe you're afraid of cancer or developing health issues in the future?

It may be the negative effect smoking will have on your looks is worrying you. You may be fed up with always "needing" to smoke and the terrible cravings and withdrawals you get when you haven't had one. Or is it how you smell after smoking?

You may be afraid of the impact smoking can have on your relationships or that being a smoker will prevent you from finding the right partner. I have yet to hear anyone list "smoker" as something they are looking for in a new partner.

If you've ever thought about quitting smoking before, you've probably got a whole list of reasons why you think it's a good idea. But let's run through a list of benefits to help you get more motivated than ever before to make that change.

The number one reason why you should want to quit.

Okay, here is the number one reason you should want to quit smoking. Are you listening? Because this is probably the most important thing I will say in this whole book.

You want to quit smoking because you love yourself. Let me say that again, you love yourself.

And when you love yourself, you look after yourself, and you take care of yourself. You only put good things in your body.

That day at the park when I had my epiphany, watching that mother with her daughter who found a cigarette butt was a turning point in my life.

When I realized, I had to love myself, just like a mother loves her child. I was my own soul mate, and I was stuck with myself until death do us part and maybe even beyond that, so I had better start looking after myself.

Your Life

The most obvious benefit of quitting is that you'll live a longer, healthier life.

Smoking is a leading cause of heart disease and cancer, and for many, it's a deadly habit.

One in five people in the United States die from smoking-related causes.[iii] Quitting smoking is the single most effective way to live longer (which is why your family wants you to quit).

Your Health

Smoking can lead to life-threatening conditions. But many don't realize all of the other health problems caused by smoking.

These include an increased risk of stroke, bronchitis, abdominal aneurysm, leukemia and bone problems.[iv]

Less serious, but just as problematic, smoking can cause asthma, bad skin, infertility, high blood pressure, sexual issues (including erectile dysfunction), stained teeth, and gums, and it takes you longer to get over a cold.

Your Sex Life

For men in their 30s, 40s and older, smoking increases the risk of erectile dysfunction (ED) by about 50%, and if you smoke 20 or more cigarettes a day, your risk is 60% higher than a man who never smoked.[v]

Unless blood can flow freely into the penis, erections struggle to happen, so these blood vessels have to be in good health.

Smoking has been proven to cause damage to blood vessels and causes them to deteriorate. Nicotine restricts the arteries that lead to the penis, reducing blood flow and pressure of blood in the penis.

This narrowing of the blood vessels increases over time, so if you haven't got problems now, things could get worse later on.

Erection issues in men who smoke may be an early warning signal that cigarettes are already damaging other areas of the body - such as the blood vessels that supply the heart.

Since smoking is so damaging to a man's sexual function, when I treat any man for erectile dysfunction, the first question I ask is "are you a smoker?"

Client Story

My favorite story about smoking and erectile dysfunction happened a few years ago. I had a client come to me to quit smoking after his wife had successfully quit smoking following a session with me. He was a successful lawyer in his mid-fifties, immaculately groomed, he radiated an aura of authority.

As we started the session, I very quickly grew frustrated with his tendency to argue with everything I said. According to him, he was in perfect health, didn't worry about the money he spent on cigarettes and, quite frankly, had no reason to quit. When I mentioned the fact that smoking was a leading cause of erectile dysfunction in men over 40, I could tell I hit a nerve.

He became much more agreeable after that, and we proceeded with the session. Around a year later, I was out to dinner with a friend and from across the restaurant I could hear someone yelling "You b****!" My friend turned to me and said "I think he's talking to you," looking like she was ready to run.

My client, the argumentative lawyer, was striding towards me, pointing his finger at me with an angry look on his face. "I can't even look at a cigarette without thinking about a limp dick, thanks to you!" Everyone in the restaurant turned to look.

"Well, are you still smoking?" I asked, with a please don't hurt me look on my face. "No, I'm not smoking! And I have to say my sex life is better than ever!" He was now grinning broadly, slapping me on the back, then strode away laughing loudly. I breathed a sigh of relief as several people asked me what I did for a living. I even got a few new clients from the restaurant that night.

Luckily, I hit the right button with him. We all have different reasons we want to quit, as well as outcomes we are afraid of, that are part of our motivation to stop smoking. Finding your specific motivation is an important part of your journey to becoming a non-smoker.

Your Finances

One of the fantastic things about quitting is that you suddenly find that you have more money. The money you spend on cigarettes can be used for other things, and this gives you a lot more disposable income.

In any case, you're throwing away hundreds of dollars per month that you could be using in a much more positive way.

Your Schedule

When you quit smoking, you no longer have to schedule smoke breaks. The average smoker spends an hour a day smoking. Once you quit, you no longer have to worry about scheduling your smokes or when you are able to fit it in. Think about how you could use that extra hour a day.

Your Addiction

Tobacco is one of the most addictive substances we know. Quitting means getting that monkey off your back. It means freedom from cravings and withdrawal symptoms. You have control over your life and your behavior, which is empowering.

Social Embarrassment

Smokers get a bad rap these days. Smoking used to smack of sophistication, but now smokers are seen as dirty, stinky people who are addicted to a disgusting habit. In fact, there's outright discrimination against smokers – some companies won't hire you if you smoke.

When you quit, you no longer have this stigma. The smell is repulsive to non-smokers. People may not say anything but smokers always have a distinct smell that is a repellent to non-smokers, like bad body odor.

Secondhand Smoke

Studies have found that second-hand smoke is more dangerous than we once thought. If you smoke at home, you're putting your family's health at risk. Although not inhaled directly, second-hand smoke is unfiltered, making it potentially more dangerous.

Even if you're not smoking around others, smoke can linger in a room for hours after you've put out the cigarette.

Your Kids and Your Family

Studies show that the kids of parents who smoke are much more likely to become smokers themselves. No matter how much you love to smoke, there isn't one smoker in the world who would wish the habit on their kids.

Studies also say that children of smokers are more prone to behavioral problems and trouble at school. It helps if you maintain a smoke-free home and warn your kids of the dangers of smoking, but it helps even more if you quit.

And finally, the best reason of all. Your family will be proud of you. When you quit, you feel like you have a new lease on life, and you have a huge sense of achievement.

Why Quit Smoking List Exercise

START LISTING ALL OF THE REASONS YOU WANT TO STOP THIS HABIT.

This one may seem straightforward, but it can be a bit difficult. You need to take your time and put some thought into this. Don't just list the obvious health reasons. You've been warned for years of how bad smoking is with hardly any effect, so you need to come up with reasons that actually have meaning for you.

Reasons people write down that will probably not help you quit smoking:

- I don't want to get cancer.
- I don't want to have an aneurysm, heart attack or a stroke.
- I want to live to see my children and grandchildren grow up.

These are good reasons to quit smoking, of course... However, they are all possibilities that could happen rather than specific reasons.

Sure you may get cancer, you may get some terrible health issue, you may die young and miss out on being there for your children and miss out on seeing your grandchildren grow up. Or you may not...

You're not likely to overcome an addiction based on what could happen. And your mind will work overtime to persuade you that it's not going happen to you.

Instead, I recommend listing the issues that you already have.

You should list the negative ways smoking is affecting you that you are unhappy about right now and are incredibly motivated to change. To overcome your addiction to nicotine, you need a list of reasons of why you are done with smoking that is unique to you individually. Reasons that are more important than your desire to smoke.

To really identify your own motivations, I want you to make a list of all the reasons why you are quitting and add up how much you will be saving each month and each year.

Have a look at the why do I want to quit smoking examples in the next chapter to help you. Read and print out from the bonus workbook or just the Why Quit Smoking List exercise and fill it out, or just write it on a separate piece of paper.

Keep it somewhere you can take it out and read when you are tempted to smoke.

Why Do I Want To Quit Smoking? Example:

1. Health Reasons

- I get completely out of breath when I push myself even just a little bit. Just walking up a set of stairs leaves me gasping for breath.

- My hands and feet are always freezing. This may be due to poor circulation associated with smoking.

- I have a nasty hacking cough, and my nose is always running. Your body produces excess mucus as a reaction to all the chemicals and toxins in cigarette smoke and could be a precursor to severe respiratory disease.

Even if I don't get cancer, I don't want to be one of those people who has to drag an oxygen bottle around everywhere.

- I'm always tired. Could it be that my body is using up all its energy trying to eliminate the toxins and chemicals from cigarettes?

2. Vanity Reasons

- Smoking causes premature aging and wrinkling of the skin. I don't want to look like a dried up, old hag!

- I'm overweight and unfit because I struggle to exercise. I will never get into great shape and be confident in my body as a smoker.

- My fingers, fingernails, and teeth are all yellow from the tobacco. How embarrassing...

- When I get back after a smoke break at work, I see people trying to edge away from me as they wrinkle their noses because I stink of cigarette smoke. I feel like a pariah - an outcast. It's embarrassing to always be reeking of smoke. I feel like I have no self-control.

- My breath must be terrible and kissing me is like kissing an ashtray. I spend a fortune on gum and mints trying to cover it up.

3. Financial Reasons

- I spend $_____ a month and $_____ a year on cigarettes. What a waste of money.

- If I save all the money I used to spend on cigarettes, I'll have enough to take a holiday in Fiji (or some other warm tropical place) every winter.

- I could use the money to pay off my credit cards.

- I could use the money to _____ for my family.

– I could give the money I waste on smoking to a charity or to sponsor a child. The money I spent on cigarettes could now be used to make the world a better place.

Get the picture? Now make your list so you can be totally clear on your individual reasons for quitting smoking.

I want you to carry this list with you to look at it anytime you are tempted to smoke.

You can write it on a blank piece of paper, do it in the workbook or use the dictation feature in the notes app of your phone so you have a copy on your phone to look at anytime you need a reminder.

Action Steps

✓ Complete the My Excuses For Why I Can't Stop Smoking Exercise. Make a list all of the reasons you can think of why you haven't been able to quit smoking.

✓ Take those excuses and break each one down in the Breakdown Your Excuses Exercise.

✓ Complete the Why Quit Smoking List Exercise. List all the reasons you want to stop smoking, keep this list handy so you can read it if you are ever tempted to smoke.

Step 3:
Identify Your Triggers & Associations with Smoking

AS A SMOKER, YOU'RE NOT ONLY ADDICTED TO nicotine, but also to the habit of smoking when you wake up, with a hot drink, after a meal, with alcohol, after sex, when stressed or tired, hungry or upset, and so on. Before you actually give up smoking, it's important to become aware of all the habits you mentally link with smoking.

This following exercise is very helpful to identify what your triggers for smoking are and breaking the associated habits.

Think about all of the things you do while smoking, and imagine instead you snapped your fingers, while you did those things. It would feel like something was missing when you went to do those things without snapping your fingers.

We are creatures of habit, and when we change our routine, it feels strange at first.

Start with keeping a diary for a week, recording every situation in which you smoke. You might find it easy to make a note in your phone, listing the different situations that you smoke and then every time you smoke in that situation, add a 1 next to it.

After a week, add up how many cigarettes you smoked in each situation.

Your list might look something like this:

After I wake up: 7
After a meal: 14
With a hot drink: 16
With alcohol: 5
In the car: 14
After sex: 3
When I'm stressed: 5
Taking a break at work: 10
On the phone: 3
Before bed: 7
When I hang out with_____: 5

In this example, the biggest habit linked with smoking is with a hot drink. My advice would be for the next few days, don't have a cigarette with a hot drink. Then drop having a smoke for a half hour after you eat. Next stop smoking in the car or while you are on the phone.

This will help you break your associations with smoking and certain activities and situations. Leading up to your quit date, try to get to the point that when you do have a cigarette, all you do is smoke, without the related habits.

Several free quit-smoking apps and websites are very helpful with tracking what your triggers are. These apps also track how many cigarettes you have or haven't smoked and how much money you save when you do quit.

The ones I recommend are Smoke Free-David Crane, Quit Pro: stop smoking now, Livestrong: MyQuit Coach or www.becomeanex. org. I'm sure there are other good ones as well, these are the ones I have checked out personally and found helpful for clients.

Action Steps

✓ Complete the Identify Your Triggers and Associations with Smoking Exercise.

✓ Become aware of your biggest triggers to smoke and start dropping smoking when you do those things to start reducing your associations with smoking.

✓ You can download a free quit-smoking app or go to a quit smoking website to help with tracking what your triggers are. These apps also track how many cigarettes you have or haven't smoked and how much money you save when you do quit.

Step 4:
Commitment - Time to Make a Vow

THE GREATEST FACTOR WHEN DETERMINING whether a person will be successful in achieving their goal lies in that person's ability to decide exactly what it is they want.

Therefore, the biggest step to becoming a non-smoker is making up your mind to do so. When you make the decision that you will no longer accept being a smoker, you have taken the most important step for improving your life.

The person you are now is the result of all the choices you have made in your life up to this moment. Everything begins with a committed decision. It's not your fate to always be a smoker - to feel like you are not in control of your habits, or that you can't have the healthy, fit body you desire. You just haven't fully committed to being who you really want to be, a non-smoker.

If you're not entirely convinced that you need to stop smoking, then you might as well stop reading right now. Being a non-smoker will require commitment and effort, and if you go into this without full determination, you will most likely fail.

Commitment... This word doesn't seem to hold as much weight anymore. We give up as soon as the going gets tough, on our marriages, our diets, our goals and making changes in our life.

We have become weak, and as soon as something becomes uncomfortable, we panic and look for any way to make ourselves feel better and distract ourselves from what we are feeling. Food, sex, drugs, the internet, Facebook, porn, TV, and cigarettes are all ways we numb ourselves from anything we perceive is making us feel bad.

When I quit smoking, I realized how much I used smoking as a way of dealing with my emotions. Except, by smoking, I wasn't dealing with them at all. I was numbing myself, instead of confronting and processing how I felt.

By committing to becoming a non-smoker, you will initially have feelings that come up which may be uncomfortable. However, these feelings of discomfort pass.

I think the Neuroscientist Jill Bolte-Taylor explains it best based on her experience after a stroke.

"Paying attention to what my body is telling me means asking? "What is my gut sense?" to an experience. Is it something that I like, or does it make me uncomfortable? Am I okay with that? How long do I want to stay like that?

From a physiological perspective, it only takes 90 seconds for that set of triggers-stimulus, awareness, emotional connection, and anxiety rush inside of you-to run its course and be flushed away.

Unless you rerun that loop by rethinking the thoughts that re-stimulate the emotion that re-stimulates the physiological response, the uncomfortable feelings will go away."[vi]

Smoking is a crutch, but you're not meant to use crutches forever, just until you are strong enough to stand on your own. Since you are reading this, I assume that you are ready to throw that crutch of smoking, away.

It's vital to tell yourself that no matter what comes up in your life, you will remain totally committed to being a non-smoker. You will not smoke if you are stressed, or if you have a fight with your partner.

You will not smoke if hanging out with a friend who smokes, or if you get drunk or whatever the millions of other excuses that people who continue smoking use.

The "YOU DON'T SMOKE" Exercise

(Not Anymore)

On my YouTube channel, I have a clip from a scene from the movie "Reach me" which shows a great example of changing your self-talk and identity to that of a non-smoker. Check it out on my YouTube channel. **Reach Me - I don't smoke scene**

After you've watched it, or even while you are watching it, repeat the line "My name is _____, and I don't smoke!" Say this over and over.

Every day we are telling ourselves who we are and what we do. If you start to tell yourself positive statements about who you want to be and what you want to do, I guarantee your life will change for the better.

Sealing the Deal

TO REALLY CEMENT YOUR COMMITMENT TO STOP smoking, you are going to make a covenant to quit for good. A covenant (cov·e·nant) is an agreement, a contract, a stipulation, an undertaking, a commitment, a pledge or a promise.

There is a great scene in the movie Yes Men with Jim Carrey where he makes a covenant to say "yes" to life, at a motivational seminar. I highly advise watching that movie or looking up the seminar scene on YouTube.

I have created a contract for you to print out and sign. You can find a printable copy in the workbook. A contract with yourself to truly commit to being a non-smoker. Print it out and sign it. You can have other people witness you signing the contract to really make it official.

Put it somewhere where you can see it, like on your fridge or by your bed, to remind yourself that you are truly committed to stopping smoking.

I recommend setting a date when you will stop: some people like to use New Year's Day, their birthday, a special anniversary, the start of the month or a Monday.

I also find Wednesday and Thursday good days since stress seems to build during the week and by Wednesday or Thursday people's stress levels are high, and they break down and have a cigarette.

By starting on a Wednesday or a Thursday, as your stress builds, you then have the weekend to relax. It's up to you on which day will work the best for you personally. Just pick a day and commit to it.

Stop Smoking Contract

I, _____, age _____, agree to quit smoking

on this date _____.

I understand that by stopping smoking, I may experience some withdrawal symptoms such as anxiety, frustration, irritability, nausea, nervousness and headaches. I may feel uncomfortable during this important period of my life, but I will do my best to keep myself calm, as the withdrawal symptoms will only last a short period of time.

I commit to stopping smoking - for myself, to improve my health, my relationships, my finances, my appearance and my confidence, as well as it being a positive influence for everyone around me.

Smoker
Signature:_____
Date:_____

Witness
Signature:_____
Date:_____

Committing With Both Sides Of The Brain

NOW, IT'S TIME TO TAKE YOUR COMMITMENT TO QUITTING SMOKING TO AN EVEN DEEPER LEVEL.

On a blank sheet of paper, write the following statement out by hand. Write your name in the blank when you write the sentence.

I, _____, commit to being a non-smoker.

Write it out two more times.

Then, switch your pen to your non-dominant hand.

With your non-dominant hand, write the sentence three more times.

Notice how it feels different to write your commitment with your other hand. Your non-dominant hand connects with another part of your brain, and writing something you are committing to with both hands helps to integrate the commitment at a much deeper level.

Switching back to your dominant hand, write the following sentence three times.

I, _____, commit to doing whatever work is necessary on myself, to be free of my addiction to smoking.

Again, switch your pen to your non-dominant hand and write the statement three more times. Take a big, deep breath and allow that statement to really sink in.

This a great exercise for any goal you want to achieve.

Breaking Up With Smoking

BREAKING UP IS HARD TO DO… Now most of you have had a long relationship with cigarettes. You have spent a lot of time together, good and bad. You celebrate with smoking, soothe yourself when stressed, pass the time and reward yourself with them.

You're basically married to cigarettes. You pay for them, live with them and spend a lot of time with them. Some relationships are healthier than others, and your relationship with smoking is an abusive one.

Have you ever had a partner that was an abusive ass but you kept making excuses for them? Or at least have known someone who was involved with a partner who treated them like crap? You tell your friends they're not that bad, that they're really nice when it's just the two of you, but your friends know that you're full of sh*t.

You know that the abusive partner is not good for you, and it's an unhealthy relationship. You defend them to your friends, but you know that you are trying to not only convince your friends, but yourself.

In the honeymoon phase of an abusive relationship, the abuser seduces the victim and gives them the illusion they are the ones in control. They're attractive, charming, and make you feel like you're the most special person in the world. So you start to depend on them and need them around. Letting them in more and more.

They fool you by pretending to be nice in the beginning, but eventually they start to take over. Restricting you, limiting you, and slowly poisoning you...

You want to leave them, but if you do, you feel sick, you miss them and everything they used to do for you. Nothing's the same without them, and there seems to be constant reminders of them. So you break down and see them again, just this once, you tell yourself.

It's not as good as you remembered but it still feels nice, so you get sucked back in. Just to start the whole cycle again. You feel too weak to end it for good, and you don't think you can make it without them, since they have been such a big part of your life.

You feel guilty spending time with them since your friends and family hate them. It's a huge burden you carry around, and you feel incredibly conflicted. And one day, you wake up and realize that you are better off without them, and you just can't take it anymore.

Something within you snaps and you know you will do whatever it takes to end this relationship and get them out of your life.

Cigarettes are the unstable partner who makes you feel good occasionally but at the same time is toxic and bad for you. When you break up, you miss them. You feel like something is missing, you toss and turn at night, and you think about them all the time. But this is normal in a breakup. It takes time to get over them.

Think of cigarettes like an abusive ex who was terrible for your health, lowered your confidence, and stole your money. They got a lot from you. You were a good deal for them, so, of course they're going to call you and try to get you back.

It might be when you're a bit lonely or stressed or had a few too many drinks, and you see them hanging out with someone else. And you miss them and all of the things you used to do together.

But what you'll find is that when you crave their company, when they booty-call you at 12 am, their voice is going to seem more desperate than enticing, and you realize that they actually never did anything positive for you at all. You were the only one that gave in your relationship, and the only thing they ever did for you is to give you something to do with your hands.

You're going to feel the craving for their company but you know it's not worth it. Remember when you feel this way, you need to stand up to them and tell to f**k off, and that they're going to have to find someone else to manipulate and bully. By doing this the hold they have on you will become weaker.

In the beginning, it's all consuming. But as time goes on, you think about them less and less. One day you wake up, and you realize you haven't thought about them at all in a long time. When you see other people smoking, you think "Thank god that's not me!" When you look back, years later, it will seem like another life.

Life is too short to spend time with people, things, and substances that only take from you and give nothing positive in return...

If you slip up and have a cigarette, think of it like sleeping with your asshole ex. Just because you were with them once, doesn't mean you should get back together. Let it strengthen your resolve to never hang out with them again!

The Break Up With Cigarettes Exercise

THE WAY I SEE IT, YOU NEED TO DUMP CIGARETTES LIKE AN ABUSIVE LOVER. Make the decision to end your relationship, once and for all.

Write cigarettes a break-up letter or, if writing's not your thing - you can visualize cigarettes like an abusive partner and imagine breaking up with them and saying goodbye.

Thank them for the time you have shared, but it's over now. You can imagine a cord connecting you to them and cut the cord or pull it out and watch them float off in the distance. This is also a helpful exercise to do with an ex or anyone with whom you have ended a relationship.

Action Steps

✓ Complete The You Don't Smoke Exercise

✓ Print out and sign the Stop Smoking Contract

✓ Complete The Committing with Both Sides of The Brain Exercise

✓ Complete the Break Up with Cigarettes Exercise

Step 5:

Nutritional Supplements

THE BENEFITS OF NUTRITIONAL SUPPLEMENTS TO HELP QUIT SMOKING

While I don't recommend using nicotine replacement products, I am a big fan of using supplements to help with the process of becoming a non-smoker. I personally found that, even after I quit smoking, I was still having issues with addiction.

It wasn't until I stumbled across the research of neurotransmitter imbalances and how to use supplements to balance your brain chemistry and heal addictions, that I really overcame my addictive tendencies.

You know those people who never get addicted to anything, or who never overeat or feel the need to drink? It's not that they have more willpower than you, they just happen to have a balanced brain chemistry. I believe this is a big part of why some people struggle with addiction and others don't.

I have listed several supplements I find helpful in the process of quitting smoking. Obviously you don't have to take supplements to quit. However, for many of us, the reason we relapse and start smoking again is because we feel so crap due to imbalances in the body.

You stop smoking, expecting to feel much better, only to find weeks or even months on, that you still have terrible cravings. You may also feel irritable and foggy headed. If you have experienced this, the odds are that you are suffering from a neurotransmitter imbalance or deficiency.

I personally give every client I see to help quit smoking a B-complex, Niacinamide and Chromium to take with them. I believe it makes a massive difference in easing the withdrawal process and successfully quitting smoking for good.

The best book on the topic I have found is How to Quit Without Feeling S**t: The Fast, Highly Effective Way to End Addiction. By Patrick Holford, David Miller and Dr. James Braly.

Vitamin B-3 (Niacin or Niacinamide)

I do believe that Vitamin B-3 (Niacin or Niacinamide) is one of the most important supplements you can take when it comes to treating addiction.

Nicotine and niacin occupy the same receptors in the brain, which is why it is so helpful in reducing nicotine cravings.[vii]

In 1960, Bill W., the co-founder of Alcoholics Anonymous, was introduced to the benefits of B-3 by Dr. Abram Hofer who had lots of success treating alcohol addiction, depression, high cholesterol and schizophrenia with vitamin B-3.[viii]

Unsurprisingly, Bill W. was very interested in trying it and started to take 3,000 mg of vitamin B3 per day.

Within a few weeks, the depression and fatigue that troubled Bill for years was gone. Bill then gave 30 of his friends in Alcoholics Anonymous the same dosage and within months, he found vitamin B3 was very helpful for 70% of the people he gave it to.[ix]

Regrettably, many of his appointed 'medical experts' did not agree with his enthusiasm over a vitamin therapy to treat alcoholism, so he was censured by AA for promoting vitamin B-3 or niacin therapy on official AA letterhead.

The Scientologists also recommend niacin to all new recruits to help detox and rid the body of addictive patterns.

Dosage: Vitamin B-3 - Niacinamide (the non-flushing form of niacin) 500 mg to 1000 mg with breakfast and lunch. You can take Niacin (the flushing form of Vitamin B-3) 50 mg with breakfast and lunch, however most people experience a red skin flushing that tingles for about 20 to 30 minutes after.

B Complex Vitamins

B vitamins help to calm and regulate the nervous system while decreasing fatigue and stress. B vitamins can also help relieve the anxiety and insomnia that commonly occur when you quit smoking.

B Vitamins are shown to lower the amino acid homocysteine, which increases brain shrinkage and may be a cause of developing Alzheimer's. It even seems that B vitamins can decrease brain shrinkage by up to 53%, and when combined with Omega-3's show a 70% decrease in the rate of brain shrinkage.[x] And we all know that shrinkage isn't good...

Your body uses more B vitamins when you are under stress. Smoking triggers the release of stress hormones in the body, while also depleting the body of B vitamins at the same time, so quitting smoking means an increased need for all the B vitamins.

Ideally start taking B vitamins at least one week before you plan to quit.

Each B vitamin has distinct benefits for the body and mind. I have listed below each B vitamin individually with its functions that are most relevant for quitting smoking.

I highly recommend picking one or more of the individual B vitamins that you feel would benefit you the most, but always take a B-complex as well, because they work in conjunction with each other. Also, studies have shown that any long-term use of one B vitamin can cause a deficiency in another. So, I repeat: always take a B-Complex.

Vitamin B-1 (Thiamine): Helps to regulate the nervous system, heart and stabilize mood. Thiamine is helpful for adrenal fatigue, increasing focus, reducing stress, increasing energy and maintaining a positive attitude. A lack of B-1 can cause depression, fatigue, difficulty concentrating and irritability.

Vitamin B-2 (Riboflavin): Vital for the production of healthy red blood cells which transport oxygen throughout the body. More oxygen reaching the brain means a greater capacity to stay alert. It helps prevent anemia, high blood pressure, migraines and is the vitamin that causes your urine to turn bright yellow.

Vitamin B-3 (Niacin or Niacinamide (non-flushing niacin): Also called nicotinic acid, B-3 is chemically similar to nicotine and fills the nicotine receptors in your brain relieving nicotine cravings. It also helps to dilate blood vessels, improve circulation and lower cholesterol.

Vitamin B-3 also boosts the neurotransmitter GABA, which relieves anxiety and helps you to relax. It is excellent for alcohol cravings as well. I recommend taking niacinamide which is the form of niacin that doesn't cause the red skin or flushing that niacin causes unless you have high cholesterol, in which case, I recommend taking niacin since it is so effective at lowering cholesterol.

Vitamin B-5 (Pantothenic Acid): Helps to lower the negative effects of stress and is vital for proper adrenal function. B-5 is helpful for adrenal fatigue and also necessary for a healthy metabolism.

Vitamin B-6 (Pyridoxine): Helps regulate the nervous system and produce the neurotransmitters dopamine and serotonin. B-6 is important for the control of anxiety, depression, fatigue, irritability and mood swings. B-6 helps to process fats and proteins and also helps to control cravings and weight gain that often arise when you stop smoking.

Vitamin B-7 (Biotin): Essential for the breaking down of nutritional carbohydrates, fats, and proteins. Helps to stabilize blood sugar levels, strengthen hair and nails, as well as helping the body get rid of toxins.

Vitamin B-9 (Folic Acid): Folic Acid is essential for proper functioning of the nervous system and reducing the chances of birth defects. Folic acid supplements have been used to help treat depression and enhance antidepressant drugs.

Studies show that people who are lacking in folic acid do not respond as well to antidepressants, and it also plays a part in mood regulation. It lowers the effects of nicotine on the lungs and protects from cell damage which may contribute to getting cancer.

B-12 (Cobalmin): Vital for sustaining energy levels in the body. B-12 also helps to decrease cellular damage. It helps maintain a healthy digestive system. B-12 also protects against heart disease by decreasing and improving unhealthy cholesterol levels, protecting against high blood pressure and strokes.

It's essential for healthy hair, skin, and nails. It helps in cell generation and the renewal of the skin. B-12 helps protect against cancers including breast, colon, lung, and prostate cancer. Heavy smokers, drinkers, and vegetarians tend to be deficient in B-12.

Choline: This crucial nutrient is used in our liver to avoid the build-up of fat, but its most important role is in supporting your brain. Choline is a precursor to the neurotransmitter acetylcholine which helps with focus, memory and mental clarity. Acetylcholine is released when you have a cigarette, so low acetylcholine is part of why you tend to feel foggy headed after quitting smoking. Eggs are an excellent source of choline.

Choline also reduces the stress hormone cortisol, which is raised by smoking. Elevated cortisol actually prunes the neurons of your brain's memory center, which is part of why our memory tends to be worse when we are stressed.

Inositol: Helps with the metabolism of fats and cholesterol. Inositol is one of my favorite supplements for people who suffer from anxiety since it raises GABA levels which has a relaxing effect.

It has also been shown to be beneficial for treating anxiety, depression, insomnia and panic disorders. Inositol has also been found to reverse cell damage in the airways of the lungs, turning precancerous cells back to healthy ones.

Dosage: B-50 Complex - 1 with breakfast and 1 with lunch, combined with any of the individual B Vitamins you feel would be beneficial for you personally.

Chromium Polynicotinate

Chromium is a mineral that is is often deficient in the soil and is essential for a healthy blood sugar balance.

When you quit smoking, your blood sugar can become lower than when you were a smoker, since you are not having that blood sugar boost when you smoke. Taking chromium is an excellent way to regulate your blood sugar, while keeping yourself feeling balanced and calm while quitting smoking.

Studies have shown Chromium Polynicotinate is more effective than Chromium Picolinate (the more commonly known form of chromium, used to treat type 2 diabetes and promote weight loss) when it comes to blood sugar balance.

Chromium is essential for the absorption of sugar into the body's cells via insulin. When sugar is not transferred into the cells to be used as energy then your body must move it away from the blood vessels to prevent damage to the vessels.

So, where does the body transfer the sugar to prevent it from causing harm? Initially, to the liver to be saved as glycogen for upcoming use. However, the liver can only store a limited amount so the surplus glucose is then moved to your body's fat cells to be stockpiled as fat.

When your body has good levels of chromium, a healthy blood sugar balance is more easily acquired since your body is able to use greater amounts of sugar for energy rather than storing it as fat.

Since it normalizes your blood sugar, it helps to control your appetite. Chromium will also help your body deal with stress as it reduces elevated cortisol levels.

Dosage: GTF Chromium Polynicotinate - 200mcg with food 2 x a day

Vitamin C & D

Smokers are found to have below average levels of Vitamin C – in a pack a day smoker as much as 40 percent. Cigarettes drain your body of Vitamin C by breaking down and excreting it much faster than normal. Smoking uses up around 25 milligrams of vitamin C per cigarette, so if you are a pack a day smoker, you are depleting your body of 500 mg a day.

Vitamin C is a water-soluble vitamin that works to sustain the health of the body's connective tissue as well as performing as an antioxidant. Your body needs to ingest vitamin C or vitamin C containing foods, on a daily basis to maintain necessary levels.

Your body does not make vitamin C on its own, and it doesn't store it. So it is essential that you take supplemental vitamin C, as well as include fruits and veggies that contain vitamin C in your daily diet.

The benefits of vitamin C include boosting your immune system and neurotransmitters, balancing blood sugar, as well as giving you protection against cancer, heart disease, prenatal health issues, eye disease and premature aging.

When it comes to hormones and neurotransmitters, Vitamin C is often overlooked. Vitamin C is needed for the conversion of several neurotransmitters that, in turn, make up our adrenal and thyroid hormones and neurotransmitters, like dopamine and melatonin.

These hormones help to regulate your metabolism, increase focus, and boost your ability to cope with stress and relax.

Without Vitamin C, we cannot make collagen, the stuff that makes our skin elastic and helps it to appear radiant and youthful. It also protects our joints and helps wounds heal. Since smoking depletes Vitamin C, this is part of why smokers age faster and recover from surgery slower.

Vitamin C works on the immune system by helping to produce anti-virals and increasing the integrity of the mucous membranes, which help us to stop bacteria and viruses from entering the body.

It's found that smokers are sick more often, which is directly related to low vitamin C levels, and the damage smoking causes to the mucus membranes.

Are you starting to see how important Vitamin C is and why it's important for you to make sure you are getting enough? This is true for all people but it's essential when you are a smoker and in the process of stopping smoking.

Vitamin C for cigarette cravings

Suck on a chewable vitamin C tablet each time you want a cigarette or make your own vitamin C spray.

You can make vitamin C spray yourself. Vitamin C powder is inexpensive and easy to find. Just find a small empty spray bottle and make your own. Just take plain Vitamin C crystals (available from any health food store, and many online suppliers), dissolve as much as you can in a given amount of water.

Spray the back of your tongue and throat every time you want a cigarette or you can gargle with it. Other ways are to suck on a chewable vitamin C, drink the vitamin C solution, or just take vitamin C tablets in the usual way.

Vitamin C will help you to stop smoking by reducing your desire to smoke, and also helps to control hunger cravings which in turn reduces weight gain after quitting.

All of these strategies mentioned above will help you to stop smoking, and reduce food cravings at the same time.

HINT: Because vitamin C is somewhat acidic, I recommend rinsing your mouth with water afterward. If you are sensitive to acidity, you can also buy buffered vitamin C powder, such as calcium ascorbate, or non-acidic sodium ascorbate, or use the non-acidic chewable form. All these types of vitamin C are available at grocery; health food stores or online.

Warning: If you are a woman and, especially if you are pregnant or trying to get pregnant, please take vitamin C with bioflavonoids and don't take large doses for long. Vitamin C without bioflavonoids can prevent pregnancy and even induce a miscarriage, as it can interfere with hormone levels.

Dosage: Vitamin C - Up to 5000 mg of Vitamin C a day. Take a 250 mg chewable or Vitamin C spray every time you have a craving.

Vitamin D

The deficiency of Vitamin D has substantial medical and psychological consequences.
Every tissue in the body has vitamin D receptors, including the brain, heart, immune system and muscles, which means vitamin D is needed at every level for the body to function.

Vitamin D activates the genes that release dopamine and serotonin. So make sure you get at least 15 minutes of sun a day or take a vitamin D-3 supplement

Dosage: Vitamin D - 1,000 IU daily for every 11 kilos or 25 pounds of total body weight so if you weigh 150 pounds or 68 kgs, take 6000 ui a day.

Magnesium

Magnesium is an important mineral for proper nerve function. It calms the nervous system and helps relieve the stress of withdrawal symptoms. Magnesium is called 'The Relaxing Mineral." Magnesium is also essential for normal lung function. It acts as a bronchodilator, which allows for easier breathing.

One of the primary minerals that become deficient through smoking cigarettes is magnesium since it's used in the body's natural heavy metal detox process. When you take in heavy metal toxins from regular use of cigarettes, your magnesium reserves get used up very quickly. As a non-smoker, you will need to rebuild your magnesium levels, especially if you want to feel relaxed.

Greens are one of the best ways to add magnesium to your diet. Kelp is the highest food containing magnesium, weighing in at 760 milligrams of Magnesium per 3 ½ ounces or 100 g serving. I recommend supplementing with kelp or Magnesium for an added magnesium boost.

Adding Epsom salts to a bath will also help you to relax and detox, as it floods your cells with magnesium. Take a 40-minute soak using 1 to 2 cups of Epsom salts. The first 20 minutes will help release toxins and the second 20 minutes you absorb magnesium.

I also recommend adding 1 cup of baking soda and a few drops of lavender to your bath to help increase the therapeutic effects.

Dosage: Magnesium - 200 mg to 400 mg, 2 times a day, with or without food. I recommend one of the doses before bed to help with sleep

Fish Oils

Fish oil is high in Omega 3 essential fatty acids. Omega 3's are an essential nutrient for nervous system health. Taking Omega 3's can help to stabilize mood swings which can be commonly experienced when quitting smoking, not to mention help with preventing food cravings and unwanted weight gain.

Omega-3 fatty acids are excellent for increasing your body's sensitivity to leptin (the hormone that tells you you're full) which helps keep your appetite in check.

Regular servings of salmon 1 to 3 times a week will aid your intake of Omega 3's. Omega-3 fatty acids are one of the "good" types of fat. They may help lower the risk of heart disease, depression, dementia, and arthritis. Your body can't make them. You have to eat them or take supplements.

Dosage: Fish Oil - 1000mg with food up to 3 times a day. Take right before you eat to avoid fish burps.

L-Glutamine

L-Glutamine is an amino acid most often used for repairing the gut and muscle recovery after workouts, but it has many other amazing benefits. It's a helpful supplement to take when you are in the withdrawal process.

106

Glutamine is very useful for reducing alcohol, cigarette, sugar and carb cravings and is often used in programs for drug and alcohol addiction.

It also repairs the intestinal lining, calms you down and is an all-around wonder amino acid.

L-Glutamine helps to build muscle, as well as stabilizes blood sugar levels so it's also a great supplement to take to prevent weight gain after quitting smoking.

Taking L-Glutamine may also help decrease anxiety, as it increases levels of gamma-aminobutyric acid (GABA) in the brain. GABA (gamma-aminobutyric acid) is your brain's natural valium. If you're high in GABA-you feel relaxed and stress-free. If you are low in GABA-you feel anxious, irritable, overwhelmed, stressed and wired.

Alcohol, marijuana, valium and heroin all boost GABA in the brain and body, which is a big part of why we get addicted to those substances.

L-Glutamine can also improve mental clarity. If you feel "foggy headed" and have trouble focusing once you quit, L-Glutamine can be very helpful. It's absorbed into the brain quickly and is then turned into glutamic acid, which is a sugar-like substance that acts as a fuel for the brain. The result is an increased ability to focus, better memory and increased alertness.

For the first 2 or 3 weeks after quitting, take 1000-2000 mgs of L-Glutamine every 5 to 6 hours to reduce your withdrawal symptoms. You can put L-glutamine powder under your tongue to stop intense cravings quickly.

Caution: Do not take L-Glutamine for extended periods of time unless you are also doing regular exercise, which will help to use up the L-Glutamine because there is some controversy whether L-Glutamine is beneficial or harmful for long-term use.

Dosage: L-Glutamine – 2000 mgs before breakfast, and before lunch and mid-afternoon as needed.

NAC (N-Acetyl-Cysteine)

NAC is an amino acid which is a precursor of glutathione, considered to be the most important antioxidant in the body. Glutathione plays a major role in detoxification and fighting oxidative stress.

It is commonly used in hospitals intravenously or orally for acute poisoning from pain-relieving drugs, liver failure, treatment of the flu, HIV infection and COPD. It's extremely beneficial and protective of the liver and lungs.

108

If you take NAC before and after drinking alcohol, it significantly reduces hangovers or even stops you from having one. Trust me on this, I have tried this technique personally. 1200mgs before you drink and 1200 mgs before bed and you wake up feeling like you didn't drink at all.

Studies have shown NAC to be helpful with reducing many different addictions like smoking, cocaine, marijuana, gambling as well as reducing habits like nail biting and hair pulling.

Warning: You do need to make sure you are taking Vitamin C with NAC, or you may have an increased risk of kidney stones.

Dosage: NAC (N-Acetyl-Cysteine) - 1200 mgs of NAC a day, with 2000 mgs of Vitamin C (to prevent kidney stones).

MagO7

If you get ever constipated, my favorite supplement ever is MagO7, Oxygenating Digestive System Cleanser by Aerobic Life. When I quit smoking, I developed terrible constipation issues. I could go for up to a week without going.

I wish I knew about MagO7 back then. I take it every night, and you just wake up in the morning and go to the toilet without needing coffee and a you-know-what.

Over time undigested food and waste can build up in the intestinal tract and colon, which can be a perfect breeding ground for harmful bacteria. Mag O7 Oxygen Cleanse works to break down and remove old debris out of your intestines and bowel.

It also targets the harmful bacteria, while magnesium works to soften the intestinal build up and remove unwanted waste.

Dosage: Mag07 - Start with 3 pills at night, and if that doesn't do trick, try 4 or 5 the next night. You can take it anytime if you are close to a toilet, I personally take 2 or 3 a night as a maintenance dose.

Supplement Chart

Vitamin B-3 - Niacinamide (the non-flushing form of niacin) 500 mg to 1000 mg with breakfast and lunch. You can take Niacin (the flushing form of Vitamin B-3) 50 mg with breakfast and lunch, however most people experience a red skin flushing that tingles for about 30 minutes after.

B-50 Complex - 1 with breakfast and 1 with lunch

Chromium Polynicotinate (not to be confused with chromium picolinate) - 200mcg with food 2x a day

Vitamin C - Up to 5000 mg of Vitamin C a day. Take a 250 mg chewable or Vitamin C spray every time you have a craving.

Vitamin D - 1,000 IU daily for every 11 kilos or 25 pounds of total body weight so if you weigh 150 pounds or 68 kgs, take 6000 ui a day.

Magnesium - 200 to 400 mg, 2 times a day, with or without food. I recommend one of the doses before bed to help with sleep.

Fish oil or Omega 3 - 1000 mg with food up to 3 times a day. *Take right before you eat to avoid fish burps.

L-Glutamine - 2000 mg before breakfast, and before lunch and mid-afternoon if needed for cigarette, alcohol and sugar cravings.

NAC (N-Acetyl-Cystine) - 1200 mg a day. Take with 2000 mg of Vitamin C a day to prevent kidney stones.

Mag07 - Start with 3 pills at night, and if that doesn't do trick, try 4 or 5 the next night. You can take it anytime if you are close to a toilet, I personally take 2 or 3 a night as a maintenance dose.

Check out my website for links to supplements I recommend.

http://nzhypnotherapy.co.nz/services/quit-smoking/the-smoking-cure-supplements/

I'm all about making things as easy as possible, and by giving your body the nutritional support it needs - the process of stopping smoking can be easy.

As for nicotine patches, gum or vapor cigarettes, you do not need any. Your body will quickly stop craving nicotine with the help of natural supplements.

It's better to not use nicotine replacement products after you quit smoking as they all contain nicotine, which is the substance you have just given up. Furthermore, a recent study claims that nicotine patches or gum do not work long term for most smokers.[xi]

This should be evident in the fact that nicotine replacement products do not support the underlying cravings or addictive tendencies that people experience when the quit smoking.

114

Action Steps

✓ Check out the supplements I recommend. Taking supplements that help to balance your body's chemistry makes the whole process easier.

✓ Make sure that any supplements you want to try do not interact with any medication you are taking. Ask your doctor if you are not sure.

✓ The most helpful supplements to take are a B complex, niacinamide or niacin and a chromium polynicotinate supplement with breakfast and lunch and suck on a chewable vitamin C every time you have a craving.

✓ My favorite place to buy supplements is iherb.com but you can find what I recommend from lots of places. **Check out my website** for links to products I recommend.

✓ Try to start taking the supplements at least a week before your quit date.

✓ At the very least, get some chewable Vitamin C in 250 mg doses or lower to have on hand. Chew one every time you crave a cigarette, once you stop.

✓ Alternatively, you can drink the juice of half a lemon in warm or cold water for vitamin C.

Step 6:
Clean Up - Preparation for Quit Day

BEFORE YOU QUIT, I RECOMMEND THAT YOU GET rid of all ashtrays, cigarettes and cigarette packets. I also recommend that you clean all areas where you smoke, and wash any clothes that smell like cigarettes.

If you smoked inside, clean your walls, carpets, floors, and windows. The yellow gunk that is wiped off is a great reminder of what you will no longer be poisoning your body with.

A useful tool for after you quit is to save all your cigarette butts and put them in a large jar. Fill it three-quarters full with water and close it with a lid. Put it where you used to smoke so that every time you want a cigarette, you can look at it and be reminded of how disgusting smoking really is.

Also, clean the interior of your car - this may involve replacing the air filter and air conditioning filter, wiping the upholstery with a car cleaning kit (cleansing cream and protectant) and leaving plastic containers (lids punctured) of coffee beans to absorb/mask the smell. That way, your quit day is a fresh start for you.

An ozone generator is also a lifesaver for getting bad smells out of cars and houses, even smelly shoes. I bought one on Ebay for around $50, and it is remarkable in its ability to get rid strong odors. After a successful fishing trip, the cooler we used to transport the fish wasn't water tight. It leaked fish water all over the back of our new car.

We didn't even realize it until the next day when getting in the car - it reeked of rotting fish. After trying everything to get the smell out, days later you still couldn't get in the car without gagging. I then remembered our ozone generator and after 30 minutes of running it in the car, the smell was gone.

We also own a beautiful sports car that had once belonged to a smoker. We had it professionally cleaned and shampooed (TWICE), plus had all of the air filters replaced. We also had hidden containers of coffee beans strategically around the interior of the car, but it still smelled of smoke when you got in it. After 30 minutes with the ozone generator, I can no longer smell smoke, even on a hot day.

Just remember to remove any air fresheners or scented candles from any area you use the ozone generator, my daughter learned this the hard way after running it in her room, and all of her scented candles became unscented!

Action Steps: Clean Up

✓ Get rid of all ashtrays, cigarettes and cigarette packets.

✓ Clean all areas where you've smoked, and wash any clothes that smell like cigarettes.

✓ If you smoked inside, clean your walls, carpets, floors and windows.

✓ Save all your cigarette butts and put them in a large jar with water and close it with a lid. Put it where you used to smoke so that every time you want a cigarette, you can look at it and be reminded of how disgusting smoking really is.

✓ Clean the interior of your car.

Step 7: Tools and Techniques

I HAVE INCLUDED MANY DIFFERENT TECHNIQUES that I have personally used and teach to my clients that will help you stop smoking.

You can also use these tools for many other issues in your life. You don't need to use all of them, different tools work for different people.

Check out the techniques and use the ones you feel comfortable with. Most of these techniques are designed to help calm you down.

I know from personal experience and with working with thousands of clients, one of the main reasons we relapse and start smoking again is when we feel stressed or overwhelmed by cravings.

The more tools you have to deal with cravings and triggers to smoke, the easier you will find it to resist the urge to smoke and stay smoke free.

What's in the Tool Box?

- The Bring It On Technique
- Healing Your Inner Child
- Visualizations/Hypnosis
- Negative Future Self Exercise
- The Future You Visualization
- The Smoking Cure Relaxation Audio MP3
- The Rebalancing Technique
- Tapping
- The 4 + 4 + 8 breath
- Eye Patching
- Vegas Technique
- Reward Yourself

The Bring It On Technique

I BELIEVE THE MOST IMPORTANT SKILL YOU NEED TO QUIT SMOKING PERMANENTLY, IS TO LEARN HOW TO MANAGE YOUR CRAVINGS TO SMOKE. When we give in, to our unhealthy desires, we stay on the addiction merry-go-round. Just because you have an urge to do something, it doesn't mean you should act on it.

1. Wait until you are craving a cigarette.

2. Take a deep breath and ask that desire to grow as quickly as possible. Continue to breathe deeply as you focus on the craving growing stronger and multiplying throughout your body. You may experience anxiety or intense feelings but deal with it by asking the desire to increase.

3. Now imagine smoking 3 cigarettes at once, and as soon as you finish those, imagine doing it again. Taste the acetone, ammonia, arsenic, butane, carbon monoxide, formaldehyde, insecticide, lead and tar you're pulling into your lungs. Really feel the 4,000 chemicals, which at least 69 of those chemicals are known to cause cancer - burning your tongue, your throat, and your lungs.

4. Imagine indulging your craving until you're sick... The horrible taste in your mouth, the smoke singeing your throat and your lungs. Feel your throat and lungs constricting, your chest hurting as your muscles spasm in protest of the poison you're sucking into your lungs. Your body racked with a coughing fit.

5. Tell yourself you can smoke, but you're going to go hard. Feel the dizziness, your head spinning, and wave of nausea washing over you. Remember how you felt when you first smoked, how you felt lightheaded, your body breaking out in a cold sweat just like before you get sick.

Feel how disappointed you would feel if you had a cigarette, how disappointed the people that care about you would be. Within a few minutes, your desire to smoke will vanish or be greatly reduced, and instead, you'll feel calm and accepting of your desire to smoke and know you will be able to handle the feelings that come up when you are craving a cigarette.

6. Repeat every time you have the urge to smoke. Your craving will vanish faster each time, usually in seconds, and be replaced with a genuine feeling of exceptional well-being and energy. This technique works well with anxiety and panic attacks, and any type of craving that you are trying to resist.

Part of what causes cravings is that your subconscious believes it needs nicotine to survive since it's in your system all of the time - like water or oxygen. By asking the desire to increase, you are telling your body and mind that you are okay. Through accepting and not resisting the cravings, you shift them very quickly.

There really is something to the 12 step program's motto of "one day at a time". Stay in the present. You don't need to commit to not ever smoking again for the rest of your life, you're just not going to have one right now.

"You can have just one..." your brain may tell you, but it's most likely that you won't stop at one. And then what? You end up smoking for the rest of your life. Do you really want to risk it?

Each time you deny the desire to smoke it will be an effort but, in time, the cravings will fade. You won't always be struggling with it. A good acronym to remember is N.O.P.E (Not one puff, ever!)

After a while, it may recur only for 30 seconds once every couple of months, but even if the urge strikes for only a few seconds, that's enough time to light up, so it's smart to be mentally prepared. At that moment, you don't want to forget how much you like not smoking.

Healing Your Inner Child

ONE THING I BELIEVE IS THAT ONE OF THE KEYS to healing and overcoming addiction is to identify what we didn't get in childhood. Addiction may stem from childhood trauma and is a way of numbing our emotional pain. Smoking, like most addictions, is a way of self-medicating.

We all have an inner child inside of us that is still traumatized from the upsetting things that we experienced. We are not just one personality, most of us have a few. An inner child, a rebellious teenager, a critical parent that puts us down, just to name a few.

You may not be aware of these different parts of yourself but they are there in your subconscious. Whenever you are arguing with yourself, that's your different parts conflicting with each other. Most of us are in abusive relationships, with ourselves...

I think it's important to recognize that the unhealthy behaviors we are engaging in, are ways to avoid feeling the pain we have yet to deal with.

Most addicts spend their lives trying to make an underlying feeling of malaise go away and trying to find any means possible to make it stop.

Cigarettes, alcohol, sex, porn, food, drugs and even anger are all ways of trying to numb the feeling that something is not quite right.

Inner Child Exercise

1. Identify what you feel you didn't get as a child:

As a child, I didn't get _____ from my parents or caretakers.

Examples: Acceptance, love, protection, support, encouragement, attention, affection, words of affirmation, quality time, physical touch.

2. Allow the child in you to grieve.

3. Transform your "critical inner parent" into an inner parent that unconditionally supports and loves you. Visualize a younger version of you and give them the _____(what you didn't receive as a child) as well as unconditional love and acceptance.

4. Love yourself. Love yourself like you would love a child. Just because a child wants something bad for them, it doesn't mean you give it to them. You practice tough love because you want to protect them. Protect yourself just like you protect the ones you love. You will never find anyone more deserving of your love and protection than you.

5. Try to find a picture of yourself as a child that you can look at. Then whenever you have that urge to smoke, imagine that child (you) asking you for a cigarette and how you would kindly, but firmly, tell them no. "No, you cannot have a cigarette. Cigarettes are bad for you, and I love you too much to let you do something so harmful to your body."

I highly recommend checking out Frieka Janssens' photos of children smoking to help with this exercise. She is an incredibly talented Belgium based photographer whose series of photos with smoking children drives home how crazy the act of smoking is. Google Frieka Janssens smoking children to see her photos.

I also recommend watching an advertisement done by the Thai Health Promotion Foundation showing children asking smoking adults for a light for the child's cigarette. It is an incredibly powerful video. Check it out on my YouTube channel. **Got a light? Smoking kids - very powerful video.**

Eye Patching

OKAY, I KNOW YOU ARE GOING TO THINK I'VE LOST my mind with this next technique, but keep an open mind. Eye patching is hands down the best technique I have ever found for quieting the mind and when you are trying to stop smoking - a quiet mind makes all the difference.

Have you ever wondered why some people are amazing artists, but struggle to add two plus two? Or why some people can understand the particulars of mathematics easily, but struggle to write a simple essay? It's all about which side of your brain is dominant - the left or the right.

The human brain is the most advanced information processor made-to-date. Learning about how it functions and ways of getting the most from it, is the key to achieving your greatest potential. While we do only have one brain, there are two halves or hemispheres (a right and a left side). These hemispheres are connected by a cluster of nerves called the corpus callosum, that pass information back and forth. Most of us tend to be either right or left-brain-dominant.

Each of us would benefit from examining our favorite brain location-preference. Figuring out which side you use most explains a lot about how you relate to the world. There are ways to strengthen the connection between the hemispheres that help you to use your whole brain, so you can change your thought patterns and awaken talents that have been lying dormant.

So, our brain has two sides, which think in different ways. Our right-brain is visual and gathers information by first looking at the whole picture then the details. Our left-brain is verbal and processes information by looking first at the pieces then putting them together to get the whole picture.

Our right-brain is more intuitive and emotional. Our left is analytical, critical, judgmental and sequential. Our right brain controls the left side of the body and our left-brain controls the right.

People who favor the right side of their brain tend to be more creative and intuitive. They see things as a whole and are interested in art, connecting with others and emotions. The right brain is connected with artistic ability like drawing, singing and creative writing, etc. Left-brain-dominant people tend to find right brained people's way of thinking vague and hard to follow, for they can be quite the opposite in the way they think.

Left-brainers tend to be more analytical and logical in their thinking and usually excel at math and literary skills. This does not mean that someone who is left or right-brain dominant does not use the other part of their brain. For most of us, even though one side may be dominant, the two parts of the brain work together, enabling us to function as well-rounded individuals.

The majority of us had an education that was very left-brained dominant. Most schools tend to favor left-brain ways of learning while downplaying the right-brain ones. Left-brain academic subjects focus on analysis, logical thinking, and accuracy. Right-brain subjects, on the other hand, focus on aesthetics, feeling, and creativity.

Studies have shown that syndromes like ADHD, Dyslexia, Asperger's, Obsessive-Compulsive Disorder may be due to right-brain dominance. Exercising your brain helps to create neural networks that rewire your brain, transforming the way you think and perceive the world.

As a therapist, I am always on the lookout for the latest techniques that will help my clients to change their lives for the better. I first heard about a therapy called Eye Patch Therapy while studying couple's counseling. I read about a therapist that had amazing results working with couples that fought constantly and never seemed to be able to resolve their issues.

The only thing he did differently from other therapists was have the couples cover their right eye with an eye patch. I found this so fascinating that I researched Eye Patch Therapy extensively and was amazed by what I learned.

Eye Patching has been used for years by optometrists and therapists to improve vision, treat dyslexia, ADHD, anger issues, depression, OCD, phobias, anxiety, and insomnia. It also helps stop negative thought patterns, resolve conflict and quiet the mind.

Your right eye's optic nerve is connected to the left hemisphere, and your left eye is connected to the right hemisphere. By covering the right eye with a patch, the left-brain activity is slowed significantly and causes your brain to send more information through the nerves between the hemispheres.

This, in turn, forces your brain to create new neural connections and helps your brain to grow and perceive the world in a new light.

Eye Patch Therapy is an easy way to exercise your brain and strengthen the connection between the hemispheres so that you can balance and access your whole brain and view the world from a more peaceful place.

If you continue to see life as you have always seen it, you will continue to receive from life what you always have. Unless you change your thought processes about life, you will continue to experience life as you have in the past. Patching your eyes provides your brain with a new outlook on life. Even when done over a few days, patching can drastically change your perspective and your underlying beliefs.

I decided to try eye patching to quiet my busy mind and improve negative thought patterns. I went and bought a hard eye patch from the pharmacy for a few dollars and went home to try it out, hoping that my family wouldn't think I had lost the plot with my latest hare-brained therapy – my pirate therapy as I like to call it.

I patched each eye while keeping the eye open under it for fifteen minutes a day. I went about my normal business, emailing, tidying the house, watching TV, and reading. As long as you don't use sharp instruments or drive, you'll be fine.

The first few days, I hated it! I want to rip the patch off my face. It made me feel disoriented and somewhat nauseous.

I figured it must be doing something if I was reacting that strongly, so I stuck with it. By the fourth day, I remember sitting with my children, doing a puzzle and suddenly being struck by the realization that my mind was quiet.

It wasn't until the chatter was gone that I realized how constant it had become. I was able to stay completely present and in the moment for the first time in my life.

I had been a person that worried a lot and had critical and judgmental thoughts about myself and others that I couldn't seem to control. I had always been attracted to the idea of meditation but could never turn off the seemingly unending stream of dialog my brain pumped out. After only four days of patching my eyes, I understood what the "power of now" meant.

I continued to patch my eyes every day for another few days, then three days a week and now I do it once every three to four weeks. I had tried almost every therapy possible to improve my thought patterns, limiting beliefs and negative inner dialog, only to find the answer in something I could do from home in a few minutes, without having to think about it.

The effects of regular patching can be considerable and extensive by encouraging whole-brain thinking. By strengthening the bridge between your brain hemispheres, the mind has quicker access to greater resources (both hemispheres). The overall effect is a decrease in false beliefs, a quiet and focused mind, and a greater emotional intelligence.

Patching can cause the brain to develop a new perspective on life. It can help you change your mind about a situation within minutes, and over time, improve your well-being and relationships.

It can reframe your past, increase the inventiveness of your thinking, enhance your emotional stability, and reprogram your subconscious mind to focus on what you desire in life.

I have seen people make amazing shifts in just a few weeks regarding issues they had for a lifetime, all by retraining the brain to see the world in a different way.

My only regret is that I didn't discover this technique sooner.

The Technique - How to Eye Patch

FOR A VIDEO EXPLAINING THIS TECHNIQUE, check out my video on YouTube. Eye Patch Therapy - Quiet the mind & access the power of now.

1. Place the eye patch over one eye (I recommend starting with the right eye since the right eye is connected to the left hemisphere). Adjust the patch to fit comfortably. Don't worry if you can see a bit of light out of the corner of your eye.

2. Wear the patch for several minutes - 10 to 15 minutes. If you feel uncomfortable or nauseous, take off the patch and build up to 15 minutes over time.

3. Place the patch over the other eye for the same amount of time.

Do this technique every day for a week and then every other day for a week and then as needed.

What Type of Eye Patch and Where to Buy One?

You want to buy a hard eye patch so that you can keep the eye open underneath. The drugstore or pharmacy or even a kid's pirate dress-up patch from the toy store will work.

I buy them in bulk from the dollar shop in the birthday party favors section. You should see the looks I get when I go to the checkout with hundreds of eye patches.

What you might experience after eye patching:

- Some physical discomfort - nausea, headaches
- A change in vision - you may want to have your eyes checked by a qualified optometrist if you notice a change.
- Clarity of thought - usually a clouding or confusion will arise before clarity.
- Lessening of mental chatter
- Reducing of overall stress

When to do eye patching:

While reading - practice reading with one eye patched, then the other, for a few weeks to improve speed and comprehension.

During a conflict with a family member - for greater positive results, both participants wear a patch (usually the right eye).

Just before any test or examination - during preparation time (to assist in comprehension and retention of material).

Warning: Do not patch the eyes during times when depth perception is important (such as driving, operating dangerous equipment or machines, using sharp instruments, knives, etc.).

Reward Yourself

IT'S NICE TO SEE HOW MUCH MONEY YOU ARE NO longer wasting on smoking. I recommend setting up an automatic transfer of how much you spend on cigarettes to a savings account. If you buy them daily or weekly, set up the transfer for the same amount on the same time basis, so you don't miss the money.

If you pay cash, put the money in a jar so you can see it adding up. Use the money to treat yourself or towards a larger goal.

There are several quit smoking apps that are very helpful with tracking, not only how much money you have saved, but also how many cigarettes you haven't smoked and what your triggers are. My personal favorite is Quit Pro - Stop Smoking Now.

The Rebalancing Technique

THIS AN EASY TECHNIQUE TO TELL YOUR PRIMITIVE BRAIN YOU ARE SAFE and helps to calm and relax you by activating the parasympathetic nervous system. This works great for anxiety, panic and the general overwhelming feelings that can be triggered when we quit smoking.

Remember, your subconscious believes that you need nicotine to survive, which is part of why it kicks up such a fuss when it notices your nicotine levels have gone down.

Finding ways of communicating with your subconscious and nervous system in a way it understands is key to controlling your withdrawal symptoms. I find physical actions highly effective for communicating with this primitive part of our brains.

- Find a comfortable position - standing, sitting or lying down.

- Close your eyes and take a deep breath. Really fill your lungs down into your belly.

- Place your hands down slightly away from your sides, with your palms facing forward and your fingers long and straight.

(When we are stressed or feel threatened we clench our fist and cross our arms over our chest or tummy to protect our vital organs and ourselves. By having our hands and arms open, we are telling our brain that we are safe.)

- Turn your head gently to one side, within a comfortable range with your chin slightly up.

(When we're stressed, we tend to tighten our neck muscles and bring our head down to protect our throats. By exposing our necks, we are communicating to our nervous system that we feel open and trusting.)

- Do one or more nice big yawns, really stretching your jaw open. Then focus on the muscles around your jaw being really relaxed, resting your tongue gently on the roof of your mouth.

(We have a tendency to clench our jaw muscles in times of stress, anxiety, discomfort, annoyance or when feeling depressed or overwhelmed. This tension tells your brain you are stressed and keeps the fight or flight stress response activated. Purposely relaxing the jaw helps to communicate that it's safe to relax.)

- Take slow deep breaths, exhaling for twice as long as you inhale – imagining you can breathe any stress, worries or tension out of your lungs like black smoke...

- Do this every hour or two if you are experiencing anxiety to retrain your nervous system that it's safe.

The 4 + 4 + 8 Breath

YOUR BREATH IS ONE OF YOUR MOST fundamental and potent tools to create instant calm. When you breathe deeply into the bottom half of your lungs, you send a message to your limbic brain to reduce stress-producing hormones and generate relaxation throughout your whole body. This technique will calm you within 90 seconds.

Bring your fingertips together to rebalance the right and left hemispheres of your brain. Inhale through your nose to the count of 4, hold for a count of four and exhale (either through your nose or mouth) to the count of 8.

Breathe deeply into your tummy, pushing your lungs down onto your diaphragm. You will stimulate your parasympathetic nervous system (and relax) on the exhalation, so you want to breathe out twice as long as you inhale. The pace of your mind tends to mimic the pace of your breath.

The Vagus Technique

THERE IS A NERVE IN YOUR BODY THAT, IF STIMULATED PROPERLY, WILL TRIGGER cell repair for any organ in your body including the brain.

It will lower high blood pressure, block inflammation, alleviate allergies, and reduce seizures. Stimulating this nerve can reduce anxiety and depression, improve your memory, release optimum energy levels, enhance the digestion of your food and even rebuild your DNA.

The vagus nerve (pronounced Vay-gus – meaning 'wandering') is a very long nerve that runs from the center of your brain, down through your chest (connecting to your heart) and diaphragm, and ends up in your intestines (solar plexus).

Research has shown that stem cell growth is connected to vagus nerve activity. Activating the vagus nerve can stimulate stem cells to produce new cells and even repair and rebuild your organs.

The vagus nerve is connected to the parasympathetic nervous system, which manages your digestion, relaxation and healing responses, and in turn can influence the health of your immune cells, organs and tissues, and your stem cells.

Eighty percent of the vagus nerve fibers send information from your stomach to your brain, so it's responsible for all those intuitive gut feelings. The other twenty percent of the nerve fibers from the vagus nerve are communicating with the organs which keep you alive (the heart, digestion, breathing, endocrine glands).

One of the key roles that the vagus nerve plays is acting as the cool-down button after you experience something stressful. The simple action of taking a few deep breaths after a traumatic experience will stimulate the vagus nerve to talk to the rest of your body, and tell it that the threat is gone and that your bodily functions can return to normal.

Deep diaphragmatic breathing stimulates the vagus nerve and so does stimulating the muscles around the eyes.

How to do the Vagus Technique:

1. Hold your finger up to the level between your eyes - around 3 to 4 inches or 8 to 10 cm from your eyes.

2. Look at and focus on your finger for around 5 seconds and then look at the farthest point you possibly can for 5 seconds.

3. Do this three times and then apply pressure to your closed eyes, pressing firmly for 3 to 5 seconds.

4. Take slow deep breaths as you do this.

By using the two different muscle groups around your eyes, you stimulate the vagus nerve. Then, by applying ocular compression (pressure to your eyes), you stimulate the vagus nerve but also trigger large amounts of the neurotransmitter GABA to be released.

GABA is an inhibitor chemical that helps to shut down "messages gone out of control" i.e. anxiety, seizures and restores balance in the brain.

This is how anti-anxiety and seizure drugs like valium work; by stimulating GABA receptors. Ocular compression does this on a "one shot" basis as pressure is applied to the eye. Large amounts of GABA are sent, widespread, to the brain.[xii]

Compare it to getting an instantaneous fast-acting shot of valium or lorazepam. You can actually inhibit or stop seizures by applying pressure to the eyes to trigger a GABA release.

Hypnosis and Visualization

Hypnosis...It's All In Your Head

"No problem can be solved from the same level of consciousness that created it." ~ Albert Einstein

GO TO MY WEBSITE TO DOWNLOAD YOUR QUIT SMOKING RELAXATION MP3.

http://nzhypnotherapy.co.nz/the-smoking-cure-bonus/

Hypnosis. The very word brings to mind, images of strange bearded men, swinging watches, making people 'cluck' like chickens and eat onions like an apple. As a hypnotherapist, I personally can't stand stage hypnosis. I think it makes a mockery of an amazing tool.

Unfortunately, hypnosis and hypnotists have long been portrayed in a negative light by television, films and other forms of media.

I truly believe hypnosis, or guided visualization as I like to call it, will change your life and is the most powerful tool you can use to make positive changes. A large part of this program will be using visualizations so that you can quit smoking much easier than just going "cold turkey".

Many people have been led to believe that hypnosis is something freaky, weird or involves someone trying to control you. You also may have been led to believe that you aren't in control of yourself during the process - that while under hypnosis, you are unconscious and unaware of your surroundings.

These and other misconceptions could not be further from the truth. People can only be hypnotized if they are willing to be.

Today while listening to the radio, I heard the radio hosts asking "What secret would you tell under hypnosis, that you wouldn't tell otherwise?" I was surprised to hear that this belief is still a common misconception about hypnosis.

People can lie under hypnosis and will not do anything that they are uncomfortable with. They will also disregard any statements suggested that does not co-align with their belief systems.

Using hypnosis techniques changed my life.

I quit smoking, lost weight, overcame my addiction to sugar and unhealthy food, became moderate with alcohol, overcame procrastination and self-sabotage, conquered low self-esteem, became confident within myself, learned to enjoy public speaking, learned to control and be free of anxiety. These are just a few issues I have overcome with the help of hypnotherapy.

Throughout history, thousands, if not millions, of people have benefited from hypnosis to help them make positive changes in their lives.

Some prominent users of hypnosis includes Adele, Albert Einstein, Lily Allen, Sylvester Stallone, Bruce Willis, Orlando Bloom, Ashton Kutcher, Michael Jordan, Ben Affleck, Matt Damon, David Beckham, Ellen DeGeneres, Tyra Banks, Jackie Kennedy-Onassis, Princess Diana, Tiger Woods, and even Mozart.

Just a few of the things that you can accomplish with the help of hypnosis are:

- Stop smoking

- Build self-esteem
- Change your eating habits
- Lose weight
- Get over a past relationship or person
- Put an end to sleep problems
- Overcome addictions
- Manage stress more effectively
- Conquer phobias e.g. (fear of public speaking, flying or spiders)
- Improve athletic performance

So what is hypnosis? At times it's easier to describe hypnosis by explaining what it is not. It's not sleeping. It's not being unconscious or unaware. It's not giving up your control.

Hypnosis is a natural phenomenon we all access every day, when you first wake up, while watching TV, reading a good book, Facebooking, surfing the net and when drifting off to sleep.

To understand how hypnosis works, I think it's important to understand the basics of the conscious and subconscious minds. You have a conscious mind that can think freely and create new ideas.

Then there's the subconscious mind, which is a super computer loaded with an operating system with programs for our behaviors and responses. The subconscious mind also controls your involuntary bodily functions, like your breathing, your heart beating, and your digestion just to name a few.

The subconscious mind does not move outside of its fixed programs. It reacts automatically to situations with its recorded behavior responses and it works without the control or knowledge of the conscious mind. This is why we tend to behave without thinking and respond in ways we consciously don't want to.

Imagine if you hadn't updated the software on your computer or phone since you bought it. They would be running some pretty outdated programs. We invest in updating our wardrobes, cars, furniture and homes, but not our minds...

Take smoking, for example; we consciously know that cigarettes aren't good for us, but we smoke them anyway. This is a classic example of a conflict between your conscious and subconscious mind. Your conscious mind is logical and understands.

The unconscious mind is running on automatic pilot, 95% of the time. Neuroscientists have shown the conscious mind provides 5% or less of our activity during the day. 5% is apparently quite high, some people are operating at only 1 or 2% on a conscious level.

The conscious mind processes around 50 bits of information per second compared to the subconscious mind which processes 11 million bits of data per second. So the unconscious mind is estimated to be 220,000 times more powerful than the conscious mind, and it's the unconscious mind which determines how we live our life.

Our life, and how we live it, is a direct reflection of our unconscious programming. The job of the subconscious is to create reality out of its programs, to prove the program is true. So we can have many blocking beliefs at a subconscious level that stop us from quitting smoking, even if consciously we really want to stop smoking.

For example, if your parents smoked - you would have a program in your unconscious mind that adults smoke. Or one that believes that if you quit smoking, you will gain weight, not be as fun or cool. Or one that states that it will be uncomfortable to go out socially and hang out with your friends that smoke.

A hypnotherapist or hypnosis recordings help you to enter that relaxed state at a deeper level by giving you suggestions to relax your body and quiet your mind. By doing this, your brainwaves slow down, your subconscious is opened, and it becomes easier to visualize the changes you want to make and the goals you would like to achieve.

The subconscious thinks in pictures and processes things visually, for example your dreams. When you tell it not to do something like smoke or eat crap food, it doesn't really get it. However, if you show it in pictures why you shouldn't do those things, it suddenly understands.

Your subconscious will reject anything that is against your morals so you are always in control. As a hypnotherapist, I don't want to control anyone. I just want to help you to be more in control of yourself.

However, since your subconscious mind can't tell the difference between truth and fiction, everything you tell yourself personally is accepted by the subconscious to be true.

We all have beliefs we reaffirm to ourselves every day like "I will never be able to quit smoking," "I will always be overweight," "I am terrible at public speaking," "I'm not good enough, smart enough, or will ever make enough money."

Whatever you tell yourself, your subconscious mind believes and goes about helping you to create situations which reflect those beliefs.

The quickest and most effective way to transform beliefs is through hypnosis, which changes them on the level which beliefs are held.

You can also use it to deal with relationships, anger, stress and anxiety. You can learn faster, advance your career, succeed in sales, improve athletic performance, manage pain, conquer the fear of public speaking, conquer phobias (the fear of spiders or enclosed spaces), and get over addictions (e.g. smoking).

The list truly is endless. Using self-hypnosis, you will create and experience dramatic results.

The American Medical Association (AMA) has recognized hypnosis as a beneficial treatment for well over four decades. In a review of literature published in *Psychotherapy magazine (Volume 7, Number 1, Alfred A Barrios, Ph.D.)* various technique success rates were profiled.

Success rates with lasting results:

Hypnotherapy-93% success rate after six sessions
Behavior therapy-72% after 22 sessions
Psychotherapy-38% after 699 sessions!

90.6% Success Rate for Smoking Cessation Using Hypnosis

Of 43 consecutive patients undergoing this treatment protocol, 39 reported remaining abstinent from tobacco use at follow-up (6 months to 3 years post-treatment). This represents a 90.6% success rate using hypnosis. *University of*

158

Washington School of Medicine, Depts. of Anesthesiology and Rehabilitation Medicine, Int J Clin Exp Hypn. 2001 Jul;49(3):257-66. Barber

Hypnosis Most Effective Says Largest Study Ever: 3 Times as Effective as Patch and 15 Times as Effective as Willpower.

Hypnosis is the most effective way of giving up smoking, according to the largest ever scientific comparison of ways of breaking the habit. A meta-analysis, statistically combining results of more than 600 studies of 72,000 people from America and Europe to compare various methods of quitting. On average, hypnosis was over three times as effective as nicotine replacement methods and 15 times as effective as trying to quit alone. *University of Iowa, Journal of Applied Psychology, How One in Five Give Up Smoking. October 1992.*

87% Reported Abstinence From Tobacco Use With Hypnosis

A field study of 93 male and 93 female CMHC outpatients examined the facilitation of smoking cessation by using hypnosis. At a 3-month follow-up, 86% of the men and 87% of the women reported continued abstinence from the use of tobacco using hypnosis. *Performance by gender in a stop-smoking program combining hypnosis and aversion. Johnson DL, Karkut RT. Adkar Associates, Inc., Bloomington, Indiana. Psychol Rep. 1994 Oct;75(2):851-7.*

81% Reported They Had Stopped Smoking After Hypnosis

Thirty smokers enrolled in an HMO were referred by their primary physician for treatment. Twenty-one patients returned after an initial consultation and received hypnosis for smoking cessation. At the end of treatment, 81% of those patients reported that they had stopped smoking, and 48% reported abstinence at 12 months post-treatment. *Texas A&M University, System Health Science Center, College of Medicine, College Station, TX USA. Int J Clin Exp Hypn. 2004 Jan;52(1):73-81. Clinical hypnosis for smoking cessation: preliminary results of a three-session intervention. Elkins GR, Rajab MH.*

Hypnosis Patients Twice As Likely To Remain Smoke-Free After Two Years

A study of 71 smokers showed that after a two-year follow-up, patients that quit with hypnosis were twice as likely to remain smoke-free than those who quit on their own. Guided health imagery for smoking cessation and long-term abstinence. *Wynd, CA. Journal of Nursing Scholarship, 2005; 37:3, pages 245-250.*

Hypnosis More Effective Than Drug Interventions For Smoking Cessation

Group hypnosis sessions, evaluated at a less effective success rate (22% success) than individualized hypnosis sessions.

However, group hypnosis sessions were still demonstrated here as being more effective than drug interventions. *Ohio State University, College of Nursing, Columbus, OH 43210, USA Descriptive outcomes of the American Lung Association of Ohio hypnotherapy smoking cessation program. Ahijevych K, Yerardi R, Nedilsky N.*

Numerous clinical studies have proven that hypnosis is amazingly effective in helping people to lose weight.

In a 9-week study of two weight management groups (one using hypnosis and one not using hypnosis), the hypnosis group continued to get results in the two-year follow-up, while the non-hypnosis group showed no further results (*Journal of Clinical Psychology, 1985*).

In a study of 60 women separated into hypnosis versus non-hypnosis groups, the groups using hypnosis lost an average of 17 pounds, while the non-hypnosis group lost an average of only 0.5 pounds (*Journal of Consulting and Clinical Psychology, 1986*).

In a meta-analysis, comparing the results of adding hypnosis to weight loss treatment across multiple studies, it showed

161

that **adding hypnosis increased weight loss by an average of 97% during treatment, and even more importantly increased the effectiveness POST TREATMENT by over 146%.** This study shows that hypnosis can work even better over time (*Journal of Consulting and Clinical Psychology, 1996*).

The fact of the matter is, when hypnosis sessions are added to various weight loss programs, the results are always better - more than 146% better over the long term.

If you have a habit which you'd like to be free of, (like smoking) using hypnotherapy techniques will help change your beliefs and behaviors at the core so you can stop struggling with your addiction and get on with your life.

Combining hypnosis with supplement support will give you the best chance to quit smoking for life! Also if you understand the science behind your smoking addiction this will increase your chances even further. Your options for using hypnosis elsewhere in your life are truly limitless.

Once you have downloaded your bonus Quit Smoking Relaxation Hypnosis MP3, you can listen to it at night before you are going to bed or anytime that works for you.

162

Negative Future Smoking Self Exercise

WHEN WE DO THE VISUALIZATIONS, one of the things I will have you imagine is a future self who has continued to smoke. So let's build a picture of a future you that is still smoking and the negative ways smoking has affected you.

Decide how far in the future you want to go. If you are young, I recommend a longer time frame, 15-20 years. The older you are, the shorter the time frame should be.

If you have children, go to a time where it's possible that they will smoke as a result of your influence. If you don't have children and want them, imagine yourself past the age of being able to have them, and have not been able to have them.

This could be either from health issues from smoking or not being able to find the right person to have them with -since smoking really limits your chances of finding a great partner.

Imagine yourself having really aged, prematurely wrinkled skin with a grey tone, yellow teeth, yellow nails and fingertips, and smoker's wrinkles around your mouth.

You may have gained a lot of weight, your body really unfit since you are unable to exercise due to your health issues. Or you may look too thin, with no muscle tone, your face gaunt, your arms and legs like sticks.

You may be unable to work due to your health issues, or you never achieved your career goals - not being able to stop smoking caused you to lose faith in yourself and your abilities.

Imagine living somewhere that makes you feel depressed. Somewhere small, dingy, and with yellow walls. I want you to make this image as vivid as possible, really build a picture of a smoking future self, living a life you want to avoid at all costs.

We instinctively move away from pain and towards pleasure. We want to make the thought of you continuing to smoke as painful as possible. Don't worry, we are also going to imagine a fantastic future where you are a non-smoker, and see your life turning out with your dreams being realized.

I have created a free mp3 download for you to visualize this negative and positive future exercise that you can download:

http://nzhypnotherapy.co.nz/the-smoking-cure-bonus/

But for right now, imagine what you would never want to happen, so that every time you think of smoking, your subconscious will picture that negative future and stop any desire to continue to smoke.

Take a few minutes to write down a negative future where you continued to smoke either in your workbook or on a separate piece of paper so you will be clear on what to visualize when you listen to the Negative Future Smoking Self Exercise MP3.

The Future You Visualization

WE ALL HAVE TWO VERSIONS OF OURSELVES. Our current self and our future self. Your current self may struggle with procrastination, has trouble maintaining a healthy lifestyle, smokes cigarettes, feels overwhelmed by your to-do list and doesn't have the greatest impulse control.

Your future self, however, has lots of energy and motivation, gets everything on your list done, loves to exercise, eat healthily and has amazing self-control.

The future you has more energy, time, patience and willpower. At least that's the story we tell ourselves when we put off what we need to be doing now in order reach our full potential. Your future self is more organized and motivated than the current you, so it only makes sense to leave the hard stuff to them, in the future.

Monday is our mantra, the day we are going to wake up and magically behave how we know we should, to be as happy and fulfilled, as we really want to be.

The problem is we avoid self-discipline and pile a to-do list onto a future self. Studies show when thinking of a future self, in most of us, the part of the brain that is activated is the part used when thinking of others, not ourselves. We actually think of our future self as a different person, separate to ourselves.

Idealizing our future self would be fine if we could count on them to do everything we expect of them. But we get to the future and our ideal future self is nowhere to be found. The more we can connect and align with our future self, the easier it is to change our behavior and lifestyle.

A helpful exercise is to close your eyes, take some slow deep breaths, relax the muscles in your body, starting at your scalp, working your way down to your toes. Then imagine a future you that is the ideal you, the version of you that you know you could be - if you only did what you already know you need to do.

Ask this future you for any advice that you need to quit smoking and what habits you need to consistently have, to be a non-smoker. Look back and see yourself behaving as your future self, now. Imagine floating into your future self's body, your body forming a new blueprint, all beliefs, all behaviors aligning with your future self now.

The Tapping Technique

WHEN CRAVINGS HIT, IT CAN BE HARD TO KNOW HOW TO DEAL WITH THEM. I firmly believe the more tools you have to cope, the more successful you'll be in stopping smoking for good. Here's a method that can work wonders. I've found Tapping, also known as EFT (Emotional Freedom Technique), to be extremely powerful.

I initially thought tapping was a ridiculous technique when I first saw it being done. But yet, I always try to have an open mind when it comes to trying new things even if I might look like a dick. I instantly felt a positive shift when I did the tapping.

Tapping is a self-help technique that combines acupressure and psychology to help relieve cravings, negative beliefs, pain, and stress.

Many of the top medical professionals, scientists, and therapists from Deepak Chopra, M.D. to Albert Szent-Gyorgi, Nobel Laureate in Medicine, advocate the importance of addressing the body's energy system in regards to healing and changing unhealthy behaviors.[xiii]

In this chapter, I'll explain to you what tapping is, how you can use this powerful tool to curb your cravings and remove the blocks standing between you and being a non-smoker. You'll learn hands-on how to tap and ways of customizing its methods for you.

You'll learn:

- The basics of tapping and how it can be applied to your addiction to smoking and other areas of your life.
- Step-by-step how to do an effective tapping sequence.
- How to identify the right phrases and beliefs to tap on that will apply to you individually.

So What Is Tapping?

It's a tool that combines psychology and electromagnetic energy flow techniques. The roots of tapping are in acupuncture which involves placing needles in specific locations on the body to resolve blockages of energy.

Energy flows through the body along meridians (energy pathways). There are key spots where the meridians meet like highway intersections. Like a busy intersection where the traffic slows and cars are hardly moving.

According to Chinese medicine, this is the cause of many ailments - the energy gets congested at these intersection points. In acupuncture, needles are inserted at these points, and the flow is released.

If getting poked by needles isn't your idea of a good time, don't worry - tapping is a simpler version that's easy to learn, non-invasive, and requires no special expertise or tools. Instead of being poked with needles, you tap these points with your fingertips, and this delivers the relief you need.

You can use tapping for just about anything, cravings for cigarettes, sugar, unhealthy food, alcohol, as well as anxiety, addictions, depression, headaches, pain, post-traumatic stress disorder, obsessive-compulsive disorder and any type of belief or issue you want to let go of.

Tapping consists of two parts - meridian tapping and positive affirmations. While you tap, you repeat your affirmations to yourself. This has a powerful effect on your mind. The affirmation helps you accept what you are struggling with, while the tapping helps to release the issue from your physical body.

You bring up the negative emotions, feelings or memories in your mind while speaking about them, and at the same time, you softly tap on a series of points - on your face and body with your fingertips.

When you tap, you send a message to your brain saying, "You're okay. There may be something bothering you, but you are safe, and everything is going to be okay".

When you tap while focusing on something that triggers you, you are doing a form of exposure therapy. The exposure happens when you think about what's causing you to feel uncomfortable. Tapping shifts your body's stress response quickly back to a relaxed mode.

Negative Thoughts About Smoking You Can Clear With Tapping

Without realizing it, you have negative thoughts about quitting smoking. They may be old beliefs from childhood, that are at a subconscious level, and you don't even consciously know you have them. Some examples of negative thoughts about stopping smoking include:

- It's really hard to quit smoking
- I'll gain weight if I stop smoking
- I'm grumpy and hard to be around when I try to quit

- I won't be able to go out and have fun if I quit
- My relationships will suffer if I quit
- Smoking is how I deal with stress and relax
- Smoking makes me look cool
- All the people in my family smoke

Do any of those statements strike a chord? If one of those sentences makes you think, "That sounds exactly like me," you're off to a good start!

How Tapping Calms Your Cravings

When you are a smoker, your body believes it needs nicotine. When it's in your system all the time, your subconscious thinks that it needs to be there for your survival - just like air, food, and water.

When you stop smoking your subconscious triggers uncomfortable cravings and feelings, setting off your amygdala, which is like a fire alarm. Your amygdala is an almond-shaped cluster of neurons at the base of the brain acting as a sensor, scanning for possible dangers.

When the amygdala perceives a danger or a threat, it sends signals which stimulate your whole body to get ready for either a fight or flight. You become edgy, irritable and unable to think of anything else.

Tapping while focusing on a craving or a thought sends the message that the amygdala can relax, even though the craving or thought is still present. With repetition, the amygdala gets the message "this lack of nicotine is not, in reality, a threat to my survival."

The Tapping Recipe

HOW TO TAP - So this is the recipe I use with my clients and on myself. There are many different ways to tap but this is my favorite way to do it.

Step One: Identify Your Target and Create A Reminder Phrase

The first step is to identify the negative thoughts or feelings with which you are struggling. This is called your target. This is your Most Pressing Issue (MPI) that is bothering you right now. You want to make sure you focus on a specific target: the issue you are working to clear. The best targets are the following:

- A symptom (a craving or physical symptom)
- A belief ("quitting smoking is too hard")
- An emotion (anger, anxiety, hurt, loneliness)

- A memory of an event (a time when you were embarrassed, hurt or failed)

Next, you're going to choose a Reminder Phrase. For example: "I'm craving a cigarette." This is a statement that you believe to be true about yourself and your situation. The most important thing about the reminder phrase is that it brings up a negative emotion or an uncomfortable feeling.

This may be a bit painful. But the truth is that we need to draw out these negative feelings of cravings, discomfort, fear, anxiety, anger or sadness, to release them.

The point of the reminder phrase is that you should feel it right in the gut. When you say this phrase to yourself, it may give you a physical sensation of pain. As you continue your tapping sessions, you'll experience that discomfort disappearing. Once it's gone, you'll find it easy to be a non-smoker.

Step Two: Identifying Your Starting Point - Your SUDS Scale

The first thing you do before you start tapping is to establish a SUDS scale. SUDS stands for Subjective Units of Distress scale. This scale helps you to rate the level of intensity of your discomfort and to be able to measure it going down.

176

If 10 is the worst your distress could possibly be, and 1 is no distress at all, where would your feelings lie on the scale?

A 10 rating would be that you feel as if you are going to lose your mind if you don't have a cigarette, and a 1 would be as if there is no craving at all.

When you finish tapping, rate your discomfort again. You may start at a 7 and then after one round of tapping be down to a 5.

You want to be at a 1 or 2 for the best result, so you keep tapping until you are down to a 1 or 2.

Step Three: Create Your Set-Up Phrase

The Set-Up Phrase is a positive affirmation that you'll repeat during the tapping session. The purpose of the Set-Up Phrase is to identify your belief, craving or pain for what it is – just a craving, fear or pain. You "put it in its place" by identifying it.

The second purpose of the set-up phrase is to accept that uncomfortable feeling. Only when you accept what you are struggling with, can you begin to release it.

How to Create a Good Set-Up Phrase

The Set Up is made up of:

The problem or issue at hand and an encouraging statement about ourselves.

The traditional phrase for tapping goes like this:

"Even though _____ (e.g. I'm craving a cigarette), I deeply and completely love and accept myself."

Into the blank, you enter the target you want to tackle. This could be something like:

- I'm craving a cigarette
- I'm struggling to quit smoking
- I want to smoke
- I'm afraid I won't be able to quit smoking
- I'm afraid I'll gain weight
- I feel frustrated and grumpy
- I feel like I'm missing out when other people smoke
- I use smoking as a way to numb myself from the fact that I'm not happy with my relationship, job, body, living situation...

And so on ...

You can change up this format if you'd like, saying for example:

"I deeply and completely love and accept myself even though I'm craving a cigarette."

If it's too hard for you to say "I deeply and completely love and accept myself," you can say "I am okay" instead, until you feel ready to start loving and accepting yourself.

The important thing is that there are two elements: acknowledge-ment of the problem and accepting yourself. As long as these two components are there, you can create any affirmation that works well for you, with any issue you have. When you apply tapping to the root cause of the problem, the relief can be permanent.

You may need to change the statement as you do additional rounds of tapping.

"Even though I want to smoke when I drink coffee, I deeply and completely love and accept myself."

"Even though I have the urge to smoke after dinner, I deeply and completely love and accept myself."

"Even though I crave smoking when I drink alcohol, I deeply and completely love and accept myself."

Saying Is Believing Your Set-Up Phrase

When you first start tapping and saying your Set-Up phrase or affirmation, it'll be strange because you don't actually believe it. Are you limiting your belief about quitting smoking? Are you fearful of being a non-smoker? It sounds crazy – you WANT to quit. At least, your conscious mind does.

And that's just it – you're not speaking to your conscious mind, but to your subconscious. At first, you may not believe the words that are coming out of your mouth, and that's okay. Just say the words and they'll have their effect.

Step Four: Start Tapping - Use Your Index and Middle Fingers of Both Hands

Tapping is the easy part. It takes only a few minutes to learn. Like all techniques, it just takes some practice.

When using tapping, we tap with the fingertips. Tapping uses the index and middle finger of both hands. You should tap firmly but lightly. About as light as if you were drumming your fingers impatiently. There's no need to be rough. The energy meridians on both sides of your body are the same.

Before tapping, remove glasses, headphones, bracelets, watches and anything else that may get in the way.

The Tapping Points

THERE ARE MANY DIFFERENT SEQUENCES OF TAPPING the different points you have. This is what I personally have found to be the most effective order, after using this technique with thousands of clients over the years. I'm not saying this is the right way and others are wrong. It's just my way. You are welcome to change it to suit you.

To watch a video explaining this technique look up my video on YouTube. **Tapping or EFT for Smoking Cravings** - How to Quit Smoking Without Feeling Like Sh*T.

The Meridian Points:

The Sore Spot - This is the starting point, saying just the reminder phrase.

For example: "I'm addicted to cigarettes."

Start by rubbing the sore point on one side or both sides from the top down while saying your Set Up Phrase. This spot is located on both sides, starting just under the collarbone to the middle of the pectoral muscle and is an acupuncture point that's related to the lymphatic system.

The spot may feel sore or tender when you rub it since lymphatic congestion occurs here. When you massage it, you are helping your body release the congestion.

Rub in a downwards motion, gently but firmly, but not so hard that you hurt or cause yourself pain. Say the phrase once, as you rub downwards two to three times and then switch sides repeating the phrase, or rub both sides saying the phrase twice, massaging downwards four to six times.

Top of the Head – now moving on to the top of the head, you start tapping while saying the Set Up Phrase.

For example: "Even though I'm addicted to cigarettes, I deeply and completely love and accept myself."

This point is at the crown of your head, right at the center of your skull. Tap with the fingers of both hands, while saying the phrase once and then move to the next point.

Eyebrows – point is located where your eyebrows start on the inside of your eyes.

Sides of the Eyes – point is located on the side of your eyes, located between the temple and the rim of bone that juts out just before your eye starts.

Under the Eyes – point is located about an inch under each eye.

Under the Nose – point located between your nose and lip, right in the center of where you'd have a mustache. The spot is in the groove found there. You can tap here with one or two fingers.

Chin – point found in the groove between your lips and chin. *Once you get to the chin point, you can shorten the affirmation to the keywords such as: want to smoke, craving a cigarette, etc...while saying the keywords three times.

Collarbones – points located just below each collarbone. Put a fist to the base of your throat where you would knot a necktie. You'll feel the two collarbone knobs jutting out. The meridian points are just below the bone where it's soft and sensitive if you press.

Under the Arms – points are just below your armpit. If you're a woman, they're where your bra strap would be. They're approximately level with your nipples.

Wrists – points are in the middle of the wrist at the base of your palm. You can tap these points with your fingers, whole hands, or by tapping both wrists together.

*On all the facial points you can tap with one or two fingers of each hand. On most of the body points, you can use two to three on each hand. Do what feels most comfortable for you.

The Karate Chop - Start by tapping on the side of your palm below your pinky, with your fingers, the palm of your hand or tapping both sides of your palms together. If you're tapping one side at a time, say the keywords three times and then switch sides, repeating the keywords. Or if you're tapping both hands together, say the keyword three times as you tap your hands rapidly.

Slowly take a deep breath, breathing right down into your belly and as you exhale, imagine you are blowing out any stress, any tension out of your lungs like black smoke.

Take your SUDS again. Continue to tap until you are at a 1 or 2.

TAPPING POINTS

MIND BODY HEALTH LTD ©

TOP OF HEAD

EYEBROW

SIDE OF EYE

UNDER NOSE

UNDER EYE

CHIN

INSIDE OF WRIST

TOP OF HAND

Sore Spot

(Both Sides)

KARATE CHOP

UNDER ARM
(4 inches from armpit)

COLLARBONE

www.carolinecranshaw.com

185

Tapping Cheat Sheet

1. **Identify your target (the issue that's bothering you the most right now) and create a reminder phrase (putting the issue into words to help resolve it).** For example: "I'm craving a cigarette." Really allow yourself to feel it throughout your whole body.

2. **Starting Point** - Establish a SUDS scale. SUDS stands for Subjective Units of Distress scale. This helps you to rate the level of intensity of your discomfort and to be able to measure it going down. If 10 is the worst it could possibly be, and 1 is no distress at all, where would you lie on the scale? On a scale of 1 to 10, I am at a _____.

3. **Create a Set-Up Phrase from the Reminder Phrase.** The set-up is made up of: The problem or issue at hand plus an encouraging statement about ourselves.

"Even though _____ (e.g. I'm craving a cigarette), I deeply and completely love and accept myself."

4. **Say the Reminder Phrase**, example "I'm craving a cigarette" while rubbing the sore spot in a downwards motion.

186

5. Now moving on to the top of the head, start tapping while saying the set-up phrase. For example: "Even though I'm craving a cigarette, I deeply and completely love and accept myself."

6. Tap the eyebrow, side of the eye, under the eye and under the nose points while saying the set-up phrase. "Even though I'm craving a cigarette, I deeply and completely love and accept myself."

7. Once you reach the chin point, you can shorten the set-up phrase to just the keywords of the phrase. "Craving a cigarette." Repeat the keywords three times, while tapping continuously.

8. Tap the following points: the collarbone, under the arms, inside the wrists, top of the hands and the karate chop points, while repeating the keywords three times on each point.

9. Slowly take a deep breath, breathing right down into your belly and as you exhale, imagine you are blowing out any stress, any tension out of your lungs like black smoke.

10. Take your SUDS again. Continue to tap until you are at a 1 or 2.

The Action Plan

Putting It All Together

1. Download the workbook and quit smoking relaxation here. http://nzhypnotherapy.co.nz/the-smoking-cure-bonus/

2. Read the Book - and do the exercises that appeal to you with the help of your workbook. You can buy a journal or write them out on a blank piece of paper. You don't need to do all of them if you don't want to, just do the ones that resonate with you. However, for the best results, do as many as possible.

I believe the most vital exercises to do are sign the Stop Smoking Contract (set a final quit date), the Committing With Both Sides Of The Brain Exercise, and the Identify and Track

Your Triggers for Smoking Exercise. You can do these on a piece of paper, your workbook, or on your phone.

3. Check out the supplements I recommend. http://nzhypnotherapy.co.nz/services/quit-smoking/the-smoking-cure-supplements/.

Taking supplements that help to balance your brain chemistry makes the whole process easier. Try to start taking the supplements at least a week before your quit date. At the very least, get some chewable Vitamin C in 250 mg doses or lower to have on hand.

Chew one every time you crave a cigarette. It really does help with cravings. Alternatively, you can drink the juice of half a lemon in warm or cold water.

4. Learn the different tools and techniques in the book (The Bring It On Technique, Tapping, Visualization, Eye Patching, The Vagus Technique, Rewards) to help you manage cravings when they come up. Learning to accept the desire to smoke as it arises and relaxing into it, instead of fighting it - is the key to successfully stop smoking.

5. Being comfortable with being uncomfortable, while you adjust to life without smoking is vital to your healing process as you recover from your addiction. Remind yourself that, in this instance, your discomfort is good for you.

6. Listen to the Smoking Cure Relaxation MP3 at a time that is convenient for you. Some people find listening at night before bed the best time, others prefer during the day. Do whatever works for you. (Do Not Listen To The Relaxation MP3 While Driving!)

7. Clean up in preparation for quitting. Clean your car, clothes, areas where you smoke and get rid of smoking paraphernalia.

8. Quit smoking.

What To Expect

THE FIRST DAY - I RECOMMEND HAVING YOUR LAST cigarette at night so it's a fresh start for you when you wake up. Withdrawal symptoms usually begin a short time after you would have normally had your first cigarette.

The first withdrawal symptoms include:

- Intense cravings
- Anxiety and tension
- Headaches and lack of focus
- Feeling restless
- Feeling tired or overwhelmed
- Increased appetite
- Anger, irritability, and frustration

Know that these feelings are normal. Your subconscious is used to having nicotine in your system consistently, so when your nicotine levels drop - your subconscious purposely makes you feel uncomfortable. Your subconscious believes you need nicotine to survive since it's in your system all the time.

Your blood sugar will also tend to be low or unstable since your body is not releasing glucose/sugar as much without cigarettes.

Tips for the first few days:

PREPARE TO BE COMFORTABLE WITH BEING UNCOMFORTABLE FOR THE NEXT FEW DAYS. Some people breeze through, others really struggle.

Remember your body lies to you, it will trigger every uncomfortable feeling it can to get you to smoke. Just like it tells you to eat when you're not hungry or or that it's a good idea to take drugs. Just observe the BS it's trying to fool you with and do something else instead.

Drink lots of water and have healthy snacks on hand.

Eat protein with every meal to help balance your blood sugar and snack on fruit, or sip fruit juice, if you feel your blood sugar crashing.

Instead of smoking after meals, try brushing your teeth or going for a walk.

If you always smoke while driving, try something else: Listen to an audio book, a podcast, or your favorite music. One of my favorites, is listening to stand up comedy on Spotify. Another way to break the habit of smoking while driving is to take the train or bus for a while, if that works for you.

Remember NOPE – NOT ONE PUFF EVER! Say it to yourself as many times as it takes. Your mind can be a tricky thing, and it will come up with every excuse possible to get you to have a cigarette. It'll tell you that one cigarette won't hurt. That logic can be very convincing, especially when you're in the middle of a craving.

Do not be fooled. Tell yourself, before the cravings even start, that you will not have even one little puff, ever again. Because the truth is, that even one drag on a cigarette will hurt you. One little puff leads to another and soon you're not just sneaking a puff, you're smoking.

Do not be fooled by the bullsh*t excuses your mind invents. A single puff will almost always lead back to being a smoker.

Remember to take a B complex, niacinamide or niacin and a chromium polynicotinate supplement with breakfast and lunch. Also have some chewable vitamin C on hand to suck on every time you have a craving.

Check out the chapter on supplements or for more info go to:

http://nzhypnotherapy.co.nz/services/quit-smoking/the-smoking-cure-supplements/

TAKE IT EASY AND REST WHEN YOU CAN.

Work up a sweat: do some exercise, take a hot bath, shower or sauna to speed up the detox process. A hot bath with 2 cups of Epsom salts and 1 cup of baking soda is great for relaxation and detoxing. Drink lots of water while you're soaking and lie down and rest after you get out.

Use the tools in this book to help with your cravings as they come up. Listen to the Relaxation mp3, do the Bring It On Technique, Tapping or the 4+8 Breathing Exercise.

Picture your reptile - telling you to smoke and say to it "I never smoke now!"

Listen to some hypnosis or relaxation audios when you go to bed to keep up the process of reprogramming your subconscious mind.

The First Week

A<small>T THIS POINT, THE NICOTINE IS OUT OF YOUR
SYSTEM.</small> The worst is over, but since the nicotine is out
of your body - your withdrawal symptoms may peak. Think
of it as if your subconscious is having a tantrum and it's
upping the ante to try to get what it wants. You may start to
come up with every excuse of why you should have a
cigarette. **Do Not Give In...**

Symptoms you may experience:

- Digestive issues
- Constipation or diarrhea
- Nausea and abdominal cramps
- Headaches and lack of focus
- Irritability and frustration
- Depression and mood swings
- Sleep issues

- Cold like symptoms as the lungs begin to clear (coughing, runny nose and sore throat)

Tips to get through:

Love yourself. Love yourself like you love a child or pet. Just because your toddler or pet wants something bad for them doesn't mean should you give it to them. You practice tough love because you want to protect them.

Protect yourself just like you protect the ones you love. You will never find anyone more deserving of your love and protection than you.

Allow yourself to feel what you're feeling. Let your cravings wash over you. As far as I know - no one has ever died from the craving for a cigarette. Cravings don't last forever and will pass. Take some deep breaths.

Name what you're feeling. Studies show that the act of naming and saying out loud what you are feeling helps those feelings to pass. The more you try to ignore and deny your cravings and emotions, the more they persist. The fastest way out is through.

Eat healthy food, drink lots of water and keep up with the supplements, especially vitamin C and B vitamins.

196

Detox and relax with hot baths, saunas, or even hot showers. Heat and sweating help to speed up the detoxification process.

Remember how your relationship with smoking is abusive. Your cravings are your dickhead ex calling, begging for another chance. Stay strong, getting back together will only create more heartbreak. You've already been through so much in your life, and I don't think you realize how strong you really are.

You are stronger than your addiction to smoking. You are a survivor, a fighter and have been through much worse than a few pesky cravings for a smoke.

Days three and four can be the worst for some people. I remember waking up in the middle of the night on day three or four with some of the most horrific stomach cramps I've ever experienced. I was so sick as I sat on the toilet, I passed out and woke up in a cold sweat on the hard tiles, shaking like a heroin addict going through withdrawals.

I managed to crawl in the shower, crying like a baby as I sat shivering under the steaming water, feeling the massive throbbing egg swelling up on the side of my head where I must have banged it on the tiles when I passed out.

I realized, how powerful my nicotine addiction really was. My aunt was a heroin addict when I was growing up, and my mother, bless her, had tried to clean her up on more than one occasion.

I can remember sitting by her bed when I was around 11, applying cool wet cloths to my aunt's forehead - as she tossed and turned, moaning, her whole body shaking and covered in sweat. Trying my best to calm her, I vowed to myself that I was never going to be an addict like her.

As I sat in the bottom of the shower, too weak to even stand up - I knew that I had turned into an addict just like my aunt. Only instead of heroin, my nemesis was nicotine.

I decided right there and then that I was a non-smoker, and I would be for the rest of my life. That being a smoker was no better than being a heroin addict, and at that moment - I knew I was done with nicotine.

You may experience something similar or you may not. But if you do, look at it as a positive turning point in your life. A definitive moment, when you realize enough is enough, and you're not going to do this anymore.

Weeks 2 to 4

THE FIRST WEEK IS USUALLY THE WORST of the withdrawal symptoms. As you move into the following weeks, they will begin to fade away.

Symptoms you may experience and what may help:

- **Cravings:** they will be intense at first, but will fade as time goes on.

- ✓ Use the Bring It On Technique, suck on chewable Vitamin C, take deep breaths, and when around other people who smoke - remind yourself of how much better you feel, how glad you are to no longer have the burden of smoking and how you will never stink like that again.

- **Insomnia:** Usually resolves by the end of the first week.

✓ Try no devices an hour before bed (phone, TV, tablet and computer screens), stopping or lowering caffeine consumption, taking magnesium, hot baths, or melatonin.

• **Mood Swings:** You may experience more emotional ups and downs. Anger, anxiety, frustration, feelings of being overwhelmed and sadness may come up intensely the first few weeks. Some of what you're experiencing is due to blood sugar imbalance and withdrawal symptoms, and part of it is due to the fact you've used cigarettes to numb your emotions.

✓ Be present and feel your emotions, allowing them to wash over you. Unfortunately, the only way out is through. If you're present with your emotions, the negative ones will pass much faster.

• **Fatigue:** Energy levels may be lower for the first two weeks.

✓ Balancing blood sugar, taking a vitamin B complex, and taking breaks while focusing on deep breaths will help ease your fatigue.

• **Feeling Foggy Headed:** Your mental clarity should come back after two weeks.

- ✓ When you smoke, your body releases acetylcholine and dopamine which help you focus and feel mentally clear. The best food source for acetylcholine is egg yolks and whole eggs. Green tea, avocados, and almonds are good for boosting dopamine. Supplements that may help are Alpha GPC for acetylcholine and L-tyrosine for dopamine.

- **Excessive Hunger:** Appetite should return to normal within a couple of weeks.

- ✓ Include protein with every meal, try taking chromium polynicotinate to help balance blood sugar.

- **Digestive Issues & Constipation:** Mild acid reflux, heartburn, nausea and stomach pain are typically gone within two weeks at the latest, however constipation may last for up to four weeks.

- ✓ For constipation, make sure you get plenty of fiber and magnesium in your diet. Fresh lemon juice and warm water first thing in the morning to alkalize the system and a teaspoon of baking soda in a glass of water is great for heartburn.

- **Cough/Excess Mucus:** This may continue past the first month, although it normally improves in 2-3 weeks.

- ✓ Get plenty of Vitamin C, drink peppermint tea, and add ginger to your diet. These are all very healing for the lungs and helpful in clearing the toxins and mucus that have built up in your lungs. NAC (N-acetyl-L-cysteine) is a very helpful supplement for clearing the lungs, always take an NAC with Vitamin C.

Throughout the withdrawal process the biggest challenge will be your nicotine cravings and the emotional roller coaster this causes you. Nicotine cravings can cause intense anxiety, agitation, anger, frustration, mood swings and panic.

The process of quitting cigarettes is difficult in the beginning, but it gets easier and easier as time goes on. Just like the space shuttle that uses 90% of its fuel the first 10% of the trip, you will need to spend a lot of energy at the beginning to manage your body's revolt at having its favorite drug taken away.

Your desire for a cigarette may feel constant throughout the first week. However, over the next few weeks, the cravings will taper off. As time goes by, fewer cravings are experienced, and they do not last as long as before. Mood swings and irritability should ease after the first week, and then gradually smooth out over the next month, although emotional outbursts may arise now and then.

You also may notice, you have more time in your day that needs to be occupied, and it may be difficult to find new ways to spend that time. Boredom and feeling restless are often the last side effects you will have to deal with. Smoking fills time and you may experience a void without it.

I know that, for myself, I used smoking as a procrastination tool. I didn't know what I wanted to do with my life and smoking helped me to numb my fear of failure. I really wanted to become a therapist and help people deal with their trauma, so it didn't hold them back. Which was ironic, since traditional therapy had never worked for me and my own trauma was holding me back.

1 to 3 Months

CONGRATULATIONS! YOU HAVE MADE THROUGH the worse part of quitting smoking. It's at this point where a lot of people slip up. One thing to remember is that your memory will change with your mood. We all tend to rewrite history - although not consciously.

Have you ever broken up with a guy or girl because they were the biggest psycho you've ever dated, only to find yourself thinking a month later it would be a good idea to call them? "I can't even remember why we broke up!" (Hint: It's because he hit on your sister, best friend, and mother all on the same night.)

All of the horrible memories suddenly fade and to a person addicted to nicotine, those very good reasons why you quit smoking go out the window. We all have a habit of rewriting history and if you're not able to spot it and expose the bullsh*t lies that you may start to tell yourself, you will be back to smoking like Keith Richards.

Remembering why you quit smoking in the first place is so important. I recommend you keep the list of reasons of why you quit and carry it with you at all times. Carry the piece of paper you wrote this list on in your wallet or better yet, have the list on your phone.

That way, you can't conveniently forget all the very valid and important reasons why you have given up this horrible addiction that never really did much for you. When you start to have cravings, just pull it out and read it. It's much harder to lie to yourself when you have the truth right in front of you.

At this point, I find most relapses tend to be triggered by hanging out with other smokers, alcohol, drug use or stress. When you're around other smokers, the trick is to remind yourself how much better you feel being a non-smoker. Smelling the horrible stink on others that cigarettes cause helps to reaffirm that you never want to smell like that again.

Practice saying "No thanks, I don't smoke!" Feel a wave of euphoria and a rush of endorphins wash over you. Before you hang out with a smoker, say this to yourself, over and over "I'm a non-smoker, and I feel amazing!" Pump yourself up, look at yourself in the mirror and practice saying no.

Trust me. People will be in awe of you, and you will be a positive influence on the people around you. If someone tries to push it, and doesn't let up trying to get you to smoke - know it's more about them than you. I always find this interesting when socializing, watching other people's reactions to people saying no to alcohol, cigarettes, junk food, etc...

Dig your heels in, just as you did when people used to try to get you to quit smoking. Don't let people influence you to smoke again and when they do, use it to strengthen your resolve. I find with every person I help to quit smoking, there is a butterfly effect of the people around them with others quitting as well.

Again, do not be fooled by the "just one puff" rationale. Just one puff almost always leads to another. Stressful events seem to be another powerful trigger for a relapse. Stay in the moment and feel your emotions instead of stuffing them down with a cigarette. Smoking will not make any stressful situation better.

In fact, it will delay your ability to process trauma, making you more likely to suffer from anxiety, depression, and (PTSD) Post-Traumatic Stress Disorder. Unfortunately, sweetheart, the only way out is through.

When I stopped smoking, I didn't have cigarettes to numb all the stuff I didn't want to deal with. The fact was I was riddled with anxiety and phobias, I was overweight and very unhealthy, and just about every belief system I had - was screwed up.

Quitting smoking was just the start. I had to reconstruct myself, to renovate the old programs that were no longer working for me. Now you have a choice. Keep doing what you're doing, repeating the same patterns - staying stuck and disappointed in how your life has turned out, or build something new.

We don't change because we feel like it's too hard and painful. But what's really painful, is not changing and knowing deep down you aren't living up to your full potential.

Taking a good hard look at yourself, and making the changes you need to make, is painful in the beginning but very quickly sets you free. Free to live the life you always wanted and experience the happiness that you deserve. Let quitting smoking be a catalyst for making other positive changes in your life.

Solutions to Common Issues After Quitting

PART OF THE REASON PEOPLE THROW IN THE TOWEL and go back to smoking so easily is that they feel absolutely terrible and don't know how to resolve those issues quickly. Here are a few tips for getting through as painlessly as possible with common issues that come up when you quit.

Anger, Anxiety, Irritability and Mood Swings

"The truth will set you free, but first it will piss you off." ~
Gloria Steinem

When you quit smoking, you may temporarily turn into a seething, angry asshole. Or a weepy, emotional mess. This is partly due the chemical changes that occur within the brain and partly due to the fact you have used smoking as a way to deal with your emotions.

When your coping mechanism is taken away, your emotions may overwhelm you and seem much more intense. This is annoying and incredibly frustrating for you, and the people around you.

These intense mood swings are one of the more common reasons people avoid, delay or give up their attempt at quitting smoking. Your increased irritability and frustration not only affects you the quitter, but also the ones you spend time with. We use this increase in unpleasant emotions as an excuse to continue smoking.

The truth is, it isn't your aggression, irritability and short temper that caused you to abandon your decision to quit smoking, but rather, not having the tools and resources to effectively manage this aspect of the quitting smoking process. Deep down, you know that having to deal with temporary irritability and moodiness is not a justifiable reason to continue smoking.

The world does not owe you the favor of walking on eggshells while you get through your withdrawals. You cannot expect people to adjust their behavior to appease your bad moods.

Unless your name is Donald Trump, and then smoking is the least of your issues. If everyone around you has to cater to your grumpiness so that you don't act like a crazy person, you're going to find yourself pretty lonely in the end. Eventually, you may realize that some of the anger that's bubbling up isn't entirely tied to quitting smoking.

No matter what the source of the anger is, it needs to be dealt with in a way that doesn't involve sliding back into unhealthy, self-sabotaging addictions that are just masking the pain you're not dealing with.

In some cases, our anger is just a subconscious program from childhood. One of our caregivers the same way.

Sometimes we are aware of what's causing us pain, other times we know we are not happy, but don't know why. You may hide the pain and bury it. The problem is that pain is not normal, and it won't go away by pretending it's not there, so we seek relief from our pain with cigarettes, alcohol, food, and drugs, etc.

Getting in touch with your pain, unhealthy programs from childhood and letting them go, will help release your need to numb yourself with unhealthy substances. There is no separation between our mind and body. The more aware we are of what's affecting us and how to best deal with it, the more control we have over our behavior, bodies and lives.

There are many different techniques that can help you access that place of peace and not get sucked into the same destructive patterns.

Hypnotherapy, Counseling, Cognitive Behavioral Therapy (CBT), Psychotherapy, Neuro Linguistic Programming (NLP), Meditation, Eye Patch Therapy, Tapping (EFT), Deep Breathing, Visualization are just a few tools that can help shift our thoughts and behaviors towards how we'd like to be.

By coming up with effective strategies to manage the anger, anxiety and irritability that's so common when quitting smoking - a smoker can become a calm, happy ex-smoker that deals with their emotions even more effectively than they did before.

Understanding Anger and Irritability

EVERY DAY, WE CAN EXPERIENCE THINGS THAT COULD PISS US OFF.

Common causes include feelings of:

- Frustration
- Feeling judged or criticized
- Feeling harassed or pestered
- Injustice, regardless of whether real or perceived

- Feeling excluded or your needs not being met
- Requests that we don't want to do or believe are unfair
- Threats to people, things, or ideas that we hold dear
-

A lot of how we react stems from our childhood and how the people around us reacted to stress. Anger is triggered in different people for varying reasons and in different ways. Something that only mildly irritates you, may unleash total rage in someone else. Anger is highly individual however, the more aware of it you become, the more you realize that your response to anger is up to you.

I considered myself pretty easy going up until I had a car accident. I had my moments of anger and frustration, but I kept it pretty under control. However, with a frontal lobe head injury (sustained during the accident), I developed a lovely side effect, known as intermittent explosive disorder. Basically, I had impulsive rage.

A few months after my accident, it seemed to be improving, however, after I quit smoking, my ability to stay calm seem to disappear. Anything could set me off, but perceived injustice became a huge trigger for me. I had always had a thing about bullies growing up. I would bully the bullies, but without cigarettes to numb my anger, it spiraled out of control.

Whenever I saw someone treating someone else with what I perceived as a lack of respect, I turned into the Incredible Hulk. One example of my behavior, occurred when I was on a walk with a friend. I still had a limp at this point, and I saw a woman smacking her dog.

I can remember this wave of rage washing over me, and I started swearing at this woman as I tried to chase her with my limp. I yelled "you want someone to fight? Let's go bitch. I will end you!"

My friend was doubled over laughing hysterically until she realized I was serious, and very quickly had to restrain me while the woman and her dog ran away. My poor friend had to push me onto someone's front lawn and hold me down to stop me from going after this woman.

Another similar incident, happened after I had gone back to work as a hairdresser. I was cutting a client's hair when I noticed the salon director was yelling at a junior staff member for not folding highlighting foils correctly.

I put my scissors down, and limped over to the salon director shouting "You want someone to pick on? Why don't you pick on me?" I grabbed him by the back of the shirt and started to try to drag him into the back room yelling the whole way.

My boss was so shocked he pushed me out of the back room and barricaded the door. I walked back to my client, picked up my scissors and started cutting his hair again. Everyone in the salon was staring at me, silent, with their mouths hanging open. My client had a bit of a smirk on his face and asked me if I had recently had an accident. I still had a limp, so I said: "Yes, could you tell by my limp?"

He said, "That, and the fact that you're acting like a person with a head injury". He said he could help me. He was a cranial osteopath who worked with people with head injuries, and was able to assist them in controlling their behavior. I went for three sessions with him, and I'm sure that man, in some way saved my life, not to mention my job.

Afterwards I was much calmer as well as being able to walk without a limp. The biggest bonus of all was that I was able to control myself from physically trying to attack people when they made me angry. However, I still had to learn how to deal with my anger and frustration when it came up, especially once I had children but that's a story for another time...

If you have ever had a concussion or head injury and struggle with anger issues, I highly recommend seeing an Osteopath who does cranial work. I never would have believed such a gentle alternative therapy would be so effective.

So what are some effective strategies to manage the anger, anxiety, frustration, and irritability that comes up when you quit smoking and just in life in general?

Here are a few techniques you can do that I have personally found to be the most successful.

- Name It To Tame It
- The 4 + 4 + 8 Breath
- Radical Acceptance
- H.A.L.T
- Tapping
- Guided Relaxation/Hypnosis

In addition to taking a timeout, counting to 10, and taking several deep breaths are also effective strategies to deal with anger as it comes up. Boxing, punching a punching bag, yoga, and even making a pile of pillows and hitting them with a bat, are also effective ways to release pent up anger in your body.

Name It To Tame It

"NAME IT TO TAME IT" was coined by the psychologist Dan Siegel. His studies have proven that naming our emotions helps to calm down the fear center of our brain and activate the prefrontal cortex, the part of our brain that helps us to control our behavior.[xiv]

Dr. Dean Ornish explains it well: "When you take time for your feelings, you become less stressed, and you can think more clearly and creatively, making it easier to find constructive solutions."

We can't change what we're not aware of. Avoiding, suppressing or lashing out with our feelings doesn't reduce their impact on us or make them go away. Becoming aware of and naming our emotions gives us the chance to pause and take a step back so we can make healthy choices about what to do with them.

I look at emotions as a form of energy seeking to be expressed. E-motions - they need to move. Saying what you're feeling in basic terms helps us to manage and control even the most volatile emotions.

When you name your feelings out loud, you help shift and release them. Which makes it less likely that they will spew out at the expense of others.

It's okay to have feelings and emotions. It's okay to feel angry, hurt, irritated, frustrated and upset. What's not okay, is lashing out in inappropriate ways at people that don't deserve it.

My biggest trigger for relapsing with smoking, was when I was angry or upset. Smoking was how I dealt with my emotions, but I wasn't really dealing with them. I was just numbing them with nicotine.

Name It To Tame It Exercise

This exercise increases your awareness by pinpointing the type of emotion you're feeling to help release it. It also may help you identify if this may be a pattern from the past.

Try saying or writing down:

I am feeling _____.

I am feeling this way because _____.

I felt this way before when_____.

_____ (yourself or someone close to you) used to

react this way when I was younger when

_____happened.

Feel those emotions and where in your body those emotions reside. Imagine you can draw the emotions into your lungs like black smoke as you inhale, and then blow that black smoke/emotions out as you exhale. Release any negative emotions with each breath.

Check out the worksheet for this exercise in the workbook.

Radical Acceptance

"Truth is like poetry. And most people f*cking hate poetry."

~ The Big Short Movie

A LOT OF OUR STRESS COMES FROM EXPECTATIONS, resistance to change and not accepting what is happening right now. Your mind is a past/future fear-based machine that is mostly concerned with survival. It is always analyzing, comparing, judging, and chattering to you about what you or other people need to do to be better, to be accepted, to be happier, or more successful.

Your mind can be a judgmental bitch to you or to what's happening in your life right now. It likes to talk sh*t about your faults as well as other people's and how useless, stupid, unattractive or unworthy you or other people are. The problem is, a lot of the things your mind rambles on about aren't accurate. Unless you become aware that your mind tells you a lot of crap, you believe what it's saying to be true.

Most people struggle against what's happening in their lives, as though things should be different. This continual battle of resistance is exhausting and unnecessary. Almost every bit of anger, disappointment, frustration, pain and upset we experience is a result of our resistance to, or disagreement with, some current aspect of our life.

It's important to remember that acceptance does not mean you roll over and play dead, tolerate an abusive situation or become complacent. Acknowledging reality empowers you. Accepting how people and situations are, right now, puts you in control and gives you the power to change what you can control.

It's scary when something traumatic happens, but years later we can almost always look back and see what good came out of it. How those "traumas" put us on a course, we wouldn't have been on otherwise: the accidents, the job losses, the ending of a relationship that caused us to change our lives for the better.

To help us get through a challenging situation, a good mantra to have is: "This is perfect, this is what I want."

At the time, every cell of your being may be saying "THIS IS NOT PERFECT! THIS IS NOT WHAT I WANT!" But looking at life from this point of view helps you to be empowered and adaptable to change and not be a victim of it.

Think back on past situations where something happened that caused you a lot of stress, but then that change led to a positive outcome. For example: losing your job and then getting a new position much more suited to you, or a relationship ending which led to meeting someone you are much happier with.

Feeling uncomfortable and having to deal with cravings short-term when you quit smoking will have many long term benefits...

More Tools to Help Keep You Calm

H.A.L.T - Ask yourself am I hungry, angry, lonely, or tired? Sometimes just stopping for a moment and getting in touch with how you're feeling and what you need at that moment can help shift your mood. Remember that this too shall pass, and the grumpiness that comes with quitting smoking is only temporary.

We tend to keep pushing and pushing, without looking after ourselves, putting other people's needs first, and eventually, we snap. I know when I start to feel this way the best thing I can do is to lie down for a brief while - even for just 15 minutes.

Accept How You Feel - A lot of us are taught it's not okay to feel angry, especially women. That we should smile and pretend everything's okay, even when it's not. We mask our anger with a tight lipped smile on our face when inside we are seething. Instead of being upfront with how we feel and

222

what we are upset about, many of us act passive-aggressive instead.

The problem is, people see right through to what you're hiding inside and so the only person you're fooling is yourself. It's much healthier to just come out with it, but do it in a way that's calm and vulnerable.

It's hard to argue with someone who is expressing how they feel in a calm and clear way, without placing blame, and taking full responsibility for their feelings. One of the best books on this topic is Radical Honesty by Brad Blanton.

Remember that almost everything is temporary, and how you're feeling right now will change even if it doesn't feel like it. Controlling your moods is your responsibility, however nicotine withdrawal has a tendency to turn us into aggressive, inconsiderate assholes.

Your actions affect other people who have nothing to do with the fact that you're angry. Yes, it's easy to give into your anger and just unleash it on the person closest to you. But it's up to you to realize when that's about to happen and stop yourself from flying into a rage and making a fool of yourself.

Sometimes it's just too much, and before we are even aware of what's happening, we're losing our minds at some poor high school kid serving us at the movie theater because they forgot to butter our popcorn. The best thing you can do in this case is to take responsibility. "I'm so sorry. I've just quit smoking. I'm not normally like this, and you didn't deserve that. Please forgive me."

Then you hope like hell he doesn't take your popcorn in the back and add his own special sauce. Every action you take has a reaction, if you scream and yell at someone else, they are bound to do the same. What you put out there, will come back to you. This is a law of the universe I have always found to be true.

Alcohol and Spending Time with Other Smokers

I FIND ONE OF THE BIGGEST TRIGGERS FOR A RELAPSE when you've tried to quit smoking is drinking alcohol and spending time with other smokers. If you're like me, and you have a rubber arm that's easily twisted, it's these scenarios that can be your biggest downfalls with regards to relapses.

Alcohol Reduces Inhibitions

One of the big problems with alcohol is that it diminishes a person's inhibitions, as well as their resolve. When you are trying to quit smoking, lowered inhibitions increases your risk of a relapse. All of your willpower goes up in smoke after a few drinks. Your lizard brain takes over and doesn't give a crap about the past or the future, how hard it's been for you to get through that initial nicotine withdrawal, or the consequences of you continuing to smoke.

To begin with, I recommend going alcohol-free. I know, I know, it sounds like a terrible idea since you want to be able to drink and not smoke.

However, going alcohol-free will give you the advantage of being able to deal with the triggers that arise, in situations where people are drinking (without the added disadvantage of alcohol lowering your resolve).

You can look at it as a health kick, and I have to admit, it's pretty entertaining as well as eye-opening to go alcohol-free for the night when everyone else is getting drunk. Sip on a cranberry juice, soda, and lime or whatever non-alcoholic drink takes your fancy.

Socialize as you normally would, while noticing and working through the triggers that come up for you. It may not be as much fun, but it's the first step in breaking the associations you have with smoking, alcohol, and social environments.

Have a plan in place for how you're going to handle the moments when you want to smoke. Head to the bathroom or step outside for some fresh air.

Use the bring it on technique or imagine your lizard telling you to smoke, allowing your desire to smoke wash over you and then feel it being released.

Creating a New Habit

Every time you successfully overcome your desire to smoke in situations that were triggers for you, you are creating new healthy habits. It takes time to develop new habits, just like it takes time for the old ones to fade. Before you know it, you'll be able to socialize with other smokers while having a drink without it bothering you.

Other Smokers

Within my own practice, the smokers that have a partner, workmates or friends that smoke have the highest relapse rate. When everywhere you look someone is lighting up, it's much harder to maintain your resolve. Smoking can be a social and bonding activity.

If you have a partner or family member who smokes, you are around smoking every day. If your friends smoke, you'll be exposed to smoking every time you're with them. If people at work smoke, you probably have smokers around you at least five days per week.

So, how do you deal with the conflicts that can arise when you quit smoking but your partner, family, friends, and co-workers don't?

First and foremost, you must accept the fact that you may be alone in your mission to quit smoking. Feeling lonely on this journey may be frustrating and overwhelming, but you must resign yourself to the fact that just because you are quitting smoking, not everyone else around you is going to as well.

Some may try to encourage or even pressure you to start smoking again. When you quit, you may be unconsciously or even deliberately placing pressure on the people around you to quit smoking, as well. They may be threatened or resentful of you quitting, and their response may be to make quitting more difficult for you.

So be prepared for the loneliness you may feel and the backlash that you may experience from the smokers in your life. Be prepared to dig deep and find your own inner strength to carry you through this journey. I find when I make major decisions in my life and I'm truly determined to carry them through, the right people show up to help guide me through my difficulties.

I recommend taking the time to talk to the smokers in your life. Sit down and let them know that you are quitting smoking and discuss the fact that quitting is very important to you. Ask them for their support and to be considerate when they want to smoke when you're around them.

Be clear that you do not expect them to quit just because you are. You can invite them to quit with you if they feel ready. But make sure you don't have any expectations of what they are going to do.

It's up to you to decide what your boundaries are in regards to others smoking around you. The only person you are really in control of is yourself. You can ask people not to smoke around you, but ultimately, you are going to have to deal with other people smoking in front of you. You can always leave the area where other people are smoking.

Make sure you have something else to focus on if someone is smoking near you. Your phone, an app, a game or a good book will help to distract you. I find focusing on the negatives when you see other people smoking really helps.

It helped me tremendously to feel that I was not missing out by focusing on how unattractive smoking is, how terrible it smells, and what a waste of time and money smoking is. Thinking "thank God that's not me" helps to reaffirm why you quit in the first place.

If you take smoke breaks with your buddies at work, you may face another type of withdrawal besides nicotine: friend withdrawal. If you work somewhere with a designated smoking area, you may have smoking buddies you hang out with on breaks.

To make the process easier, I recommend not spending time in the smoking area. This may trigger a severe case of FOMO (fear of missing out), but you can hang out with these people at other times.

Eventually, it won't even bother you to see other people smoking; you just feel sorry for them. The first month is usually the hardest and hanging out with smokers is like a newly clean heroin addict hanging out with people that are shooting up. Not helpful.

Quitting smoking even when other people around you smoke doesn't have to be difficult and may even inspire others to stop smoking as well. Take some time to let people know that you are quitting and that you would appreciate their support.

At the same time, be thoughtful of the other smokers and allow them their freedom to smoke if they choose. Instead of telling people they shouldn't smoke, tell them to go have a cigarette.

Most smokers are rebellious at heart and reverse psychology works well. Regardless if your family, friends, and co-workers are smokers, you can quit and be an inspiration to help others quit smoking as well.

Recap

- Alcohol diminishes your inhibitions as well as your resolve, so try to avoid drinking the first month if you can.

- If you do have a drink and want a cigarette, imagine how it would taste like an ashtray was poured into your drink and make you feel sick.

- Accept the fact that you may be alone in your mission to quit smoking, but know you will be better off and will be a positive influence for others.

- Make sure you have something else to focus on if someone is smoking near you, like your phone, an app, a game or a good book to help distract you.

- Focus on the negatives when you see other people smoking. Focus on how unattractive smoking is, how terrible it smells, and what a waste of time and money smoking is.

Constipation

I NEVER KNEW WHAT IT WAS LIKE TO BE CONSTIPATED UNTIL I QUIT SMOKING. My morning coffee and cigarette kept me regular even when I treated my body like crap. Constipation, when you quit smoking, is caused by a decrease in your intestinal movements for a short period, as your body adjusts to not having nicotine to stimulate it.

It typically lasts for several weeks.

Things you can do to counteract constipation:

Hot water and fresh lemon juice first thing in the morning stimulates your liver and bowel into releasing toxins. Add a tablespoon of olive oil if you are really backed up. (Only take the olive oil on an empty stomach or else it doesn't work.)

Go for walks, do yoga, or some other type of physical activity.

Drink plenty of water (at least 6-8 glasses of daily). A new study has shown that drinking 16 ounces before meals can lead to a weight loss on average of 4.3 kg, or 9 pounds, over 12 weeks.[xv] This technique is perfect for counteracting weight gain that can occur after quitting smoking.[xvi]

Add fiber (fruits, vegetables, oats, flaxseeds, chia seeds, psyllium husks) to your diet, since it acts as an internal broom sweeping out the toxins. Fiber is also very helpful for weight loss and flushing out excess estrogens that cause hormonal imbalances.

Try drinking 1 tablespoon of psyllium husks (the main ingredient in Metamucil) added to a large glass of water. Drink another glass of water straight afterward, to make sure the psyllium doesn't absorb too much water as it passes through your digestive system. You can build up to a dosage of three times a day. Make sure you down it quickly, otherwise it's like trying to drink sludge.

Now if you're really hard-core like me, you can buy some bentonite clay, liquid or powder and add a teaspoon of that to the psyllium husks and water. The combination of bentonite clay and psyllium husks is one of most powerful detoxes I've ever used.

WARNING: BENTONITE CLAY AND PSYLLIUM HUSKS MAY CAUSE YOUR EXCREMENT TO LOOK LIKE BLACK SEAWEED. THIS IS DUE TO

What is mucoid plaque? Your intestines produce mucus to protect themselves as a self-defense. As the mucus collects over the years due to unhealthy eating and a sluggish colon, it produces a dark, sticky, and rubbery-textured substance.

This seaweed-like substance is the mucoid plaque and consists of mucus, undigested food, fecal matter, parasites, bacteria, and toxins. Ewww!

Finally, if you do get constipated, my favorite supplement is MagO7. This is not a laxative but brings in oxygen into the body to help remove old matter.

Mag O7 Oxygen Cleanse works to break down and remove old debris and targets the harmful bacteria in your gut, while the magnesium it contains works to soften the intestinal build up and remove unwanted waste.

Dizziness and Headaches

A S YOUR BODY BEGINS TO GET MORE OXYGEN, you may experience dizziness and headaches. The body is receiving more oxygen through the blood, triggering a condition that resembles hyperventilation. The headaches are partly due to the blood vessels in your head dilating. The same symptoms may occur when you have quit drinking coffee after drinking it daily.

Tips for managing the dizziness and headaches:

- Take a few slow, deep breaths (like yawning), and stretch.

- Ice packs, cold gel packs or a cloth damp with cold water (place it in the freezer for ten minutes for a homemade ice pack) placed on the forehead or

- wrapped around the back of the neck helps to reduce headaches.
- Even better, apply ice packs to your head while soaking in a warm bath with Epsom salts, baking soda and a few drops of lavender.

- Rub a few drops of lavender oil or peppermint oil on your temples and forehead. You can dilute two to three drops of lavender or peppermint oil with coconut or massage oil and rub it into the shoulders, back of neck, forehead, and temples to help reduce pain and relieve tension.

If the headaches are extreme or do not go away, seek medical advice.

Use painkillers such as Tylenol, Paracetamol or Excedrin as directed. A painkiller with caffeine, like Excedrin, is helpful during the day since it helps to constrict the blood vessels that are partly causing the headache. This is not ideal, but taking something to relieve the pain is still healthier than smoking.

Remember that this headache is caused by increased blood flow to your brain and improved circulation. Increased blood flow is a good thing for your health, your cognitive function and for healthy glowing skin. Remember, the headaches will pass normally after the first week.

Excessive Hunger

YOUR BLOOD SUGAR CAN CRASH WHEN YOU FIRST QUIT SMOKING. Many of the side effects experienced during the first week can often be traced back to low blood sugar.

Symptoms such as dizziness, headache, lack of focus, and the ravenous hunger experienced by many after quitting smoking, is often caused by this blood sugar drop. Sugar is the brain's favorite fuel, and when it's low, your brain cannot perform at its optimum level.

Your low blood sugar after quitting smoking is caused by no longer having the stimulating effect of nicotine on your blood sugar. Cigarettes cause the liver to release its stores of sugar and fat.

That's part of how how smoking works as an appetite suppressant, as well as affecting the satiety centers of your brain in your hypothalamus. When it comes to blood sugar levels, nicotine works much quicker than food.

If you use food to raise blood sugar levels, it takes up to 20 minutes from the time you chew and swallow the food before it is absorbed and released into the bloodstream, and in turn, fuels the brain.

Cigarettes cause the body to release its stores of sugar, not in 20 minutes but within seconds. When you smoke on a regular basis, your body doesn't have to release as much sugar on its own, as you do it more often by using nicotine.

This is why people tend to binge on food when they quit. They experience a drop in blood sugar and want to eat to help themselves feel better, especially something sweet.

However, even after finishing their food, they still feel like crap. It only takes a few minutes to eat, but your blood sugar takes 20 minutes, on average, after the first swallow to be raised.

Since you still don't feel better immediately, you eat a little more. Some people will keep eating until they finally start to feel better as their blood sugar stabilizes. This is part of why we tend to keep eating even though we feel full.

By the third or fourth day, your body will adjust and start to release glucose/sugar as it's needed, but you won't have the regular doses of nicotine to give you a boost without eating.

Tips for balancing your blood sugar and not gaining weight:

Eat protein with every meal to help balance your blood sugar and snack on fruit if you feel your blood sugar crashing the first few days after smoking.

If you are experiencing significantly low blood sugar, try sipping on unsweetened fruit juices like apple, blueberry, cranberry, orange, grape, and pomegranate. Adding juice to soda water and ice helps to dilute it. After the fourth day, though, this should no longer be necessary as your body will start to release sugar stores like it did before.

Make sure you eat slow-release complex carbs, like berries, melons, cherries, apples, plums, pears, sweet potatoes, yams, or quinoa to help keep your blood sugar balanced.

Try to time eating fast-release carbs within 30 minutes of finishing a resistance-training workout for the biggest benefit. You may find it helpful to change your eating patterns to one that's more consistent.

This doesn't mean you need to eat more, but it may help to redistribute the food you eat to smaller, more regular meals so that your blood sugar stays consistent throughout the day.

If you continue to have issues that are symptomatic of low blood sugar beyond day five, it may be a good time to get some nutritional advice from a professional. I highly recommend The Blood Sugar Solution by Dr. Mark Hyman and Choose to Lose: The 7-Day Carb Cycle Solution by Chris Powell.

This is the perfect time to focus on your health and fitness. You will have the energy and time to create healthier habits and a much healthier body. Remember the average smoker spends an hour a day smoking. This time is spent on a habit you have formed.

Imagine how amazing you will feel, not to mention look, if you had the habit of spending an hour a day focusing on eating healthy and exercising.

The truth is, we are a sum of our habits. Our habits are developed behaviors through frequent repetition. Most people aren't aware of their habits and don't focus on creating healthy ones. This is a shame since your habits can make or break you.

My #1 tip to balance blood sugar - Avoid any carbs that are white.

Avoiding non-organic white carbohydrates is a good place to start. I recommend cutting out all bread, cereal, pasta, tortillas, and fried foods with a crumb coating.

One reason to avoid white processed foods is chlorine dioxide, one of the chemicals that's used to bleach food even when it's made brown after.

When chlorine dioxide is combined with the protein in wheat, it forms the toxin alloxan which is known to attack the pancreas, reducing its ability to produce insulin.

Researchers are well aware of this connection and use alloxan in lab rats to induce diabetes.[xvii] Did you catch that? It's used to induce diabetes! This is terrible news if you eat anything white or "enriched." Most whole wheat bread uses white flour as a base.

Another very important reason you should cut out white carbs or choose only organic products is that most wheat, buckwheat, canola, corn, flax, lentils, oats, peas, soy, rye, potatoes, sugar beets and sunflower crops are now sprayed with a weed killer (glyphosate) before it's harvested.[xviii]

Although the makers of glyphosate claim that it's safe for human consumption, its use has skyrocketed along with connected health issues.[xix]

The manufacturers of glyphosate claim that it's not harmful to humans and animals because what it kills in plants is absent in animals. However, what glyphosate kills in plants is present in our bacteria, and this is crucial to comprehending how it's causing extensive systemic harm in humans, as well as animals.

You have up to 10 times more bacteria in your body than cells. For every type of cell in your body, you have ten microbes of various kinds; they are all affected negatively by glyphosate. Glyphosate is thought to cause a severe disturbance in our bacteria's health and life cycle.

Even worse, glyphosate affects the good bacteria first, allowing more harmful pathogens to overgrow and take over.[xx]

Scientists are finding our gut bacteria may be one of the biggest factors when it comes to maintaining a healthy weight and general health.[xxi]

So the moral of the story is.... don't eat white stuff unless you want to gain weight and try to eat organic when you can.

Insomnia

INSOMNIA IS SOMETHING THAT AFFECTS ALMOST
EVERYONE AT SOME POINT IN THEIR LIVES. They use
sleep deprivation as a torture method for a reason. Because
it will drive you crazy... Insomnia is a very common side
effect when you quit smoking.

Here are some tips on how to deal with it.

1. Cut out or lower your caffeine consumption.

Everyone knows that caffeine is a stimulant but what you
may not know, is that smokers metabolize caffeine at twice
the rate of non-smoker.[xxii] That means it's out of your system
faster. So when you're a non-smoker, you are much more
sensitive to caffeine and much more likely to feel anxious and
jittery from a dose you used to tolerate easily before.

Try replacing coffee with green tea or reducing your caffeine consumption by half.

2. Turn off electronics at least an hour before bedtime.

Most electronic devices emit a blue light that lowers your natural melatonin production. This, in turn, makes you less sleepy at night. I know, I know, we are all addicted to our screens. Unfortunately, our biology has not caught up with our love of technology.

Apple has come out with the night shift feature, which automatically changes the colors in your display to the warmer end of the spectrum when it's sunset in your location. I'm sure Android manufacturers have come out with something similar, just be aware of the effect that screens have on your biology.

3. Take a warm bath or shower at night.

Your body temperature naturally drops at night, starting around two hours before you fall asleep and bottoming out at 4 a.m. or 5 a.m. By raising your temperature, a degree or two with a bath, the drop afterward is more likely to put you into a deep sleep faster. A shower is not as effective but does help.

One to two hours before bed, try soaking in the tub for 20 to 40 minutes. Even better, add 2 cups of Epsom salts, 1 cup of baking soda and ten drops of lavender. Make sure you drink plenty of water.

Adding Epsom salts which are made of magnesium and sulfate to a bath will also help you to relax and detox, as it floods your cells with magnesium.

The lavender oil helps relax your nervous system and lower cortisol and the baking soda (sodium bicarbonate), promotes detoxification, and alkalinizes your body.

4. Take magnesium and/or melatonin before bed.

In the evening, your body releases melatonin, which makes you feel sleepy - but it only releases it if it receives the right signals from your environment.

Melatonin is known as the hormone of darkness, so your body doesn't want to release it until the lights go down. You want to transition to low light as early as 8 or 9 pm. Keeping the lights dim before bed cues your brain for sleep.

Ideally, try and get 8 hours sleep each night. You also should try to have lights out by 10:30 pm.

Our body releases a hit of cortisol (a stress hormone) at 11:00 pm, this is why some people seem to get a second wind and can struggle to get to sleep if they are up late. Cortisol can promote weight gain, particularly around the abdomen, and excess cortisol also stalls progress on weight loss.

Hey There Non-Smoker

WELCOME TO YOUR NEW LIFE. ARE YOU EXCITED? You should be. From here on out, everything in your life is going to get better. Your skin will become smoother, clearer and regain its glow.

Your teeth will become whiter, your gums healthier, and your breath will no longer smell like an ashtray. You will have more energy, sleep more deeply and feel more relaxed.

This huge burden is going to be lifted from you and it's going to be such a relief to be free of the hassle of smoking. Personally, I have never looked back, and I don't know a single person who has quit smoking that wishes they were still addicted to nicotine. For you, this is not the end but the beginning of a new life.

So my question is: What are you going to do with this fresh start? If you can quit smoking, what else can you achieve? Quitting smoking was a huge catalyst for change in my life. The time and money I saved by not smoking gave me the energy to look at other areas of my life that needed improvement and the extra money to sort them out.

Think about how much you have survived in your life. Don't save your best for some other time, give your best now. Will it be easy? Nope. Will it be worth it? Absolutely.

Resources

To download the bonus MP3 and workbook go to:

http://nzhypnotherapy.co.nz/the-smoking-cure-bonus/

For the tapping video instructions go to:
http://nzhypnotherapy.co.nz/tapping-for-quitting-smoking/

Supplement Links
http://nzhypnotherapy.co.nz/services/quit-smoking/the-smoking-cure-supplements/

Caroline's website   http://www.carolinecranshaw.com/

Caroline's Facebook page
https://www.facebook.com/Caroline-Cranshaw-143595375659280/

The Smoking Cure Facebook page
https://www.facebook.com/The-Smoking-Cure-1006705076087265/

Caroline's Instagram: mindbodyhealthstore   or carolinecranshaw

About the Author

CAROLINE IS A HYPNOTHERAPIST AND ADDICTION SPECIALIST, obsessed with helping people quit smoking as well as healing whatever other issues they may have. She lives in Auckland, New Zealand with her husband to be and is being slowly driven crazy by her blended family of five children.

Caroline grew up with a passion for health - mental and physical. Studying Psychology and Nutrition at University, she became disillusioned with the results of traditional therapy. After a visit to a hypnotherapist, Caroline realized that hypnosis combined with therapy could access deep issues and clear them in just a few sessions.

Caroline's qualifications include a Diploma in Advanced Clinical Hypnotherapy, Counseling, NLP, Parts Therapy, and Transforming Therapy. She is also a Life Coach, Food

Psychology Coach, Nutritional Therapist, a Clinical Weight Loss Coach and a self-confessed know it all.

She has studied psychology, nutrition, fitness, kinesiology, spirituality, energy medicine and consciousness extensively and makes a point of continually developing her skills and knowledge in order to ensure that her clients benefit from the most effective and rapid resolution of their issues as possible.

When not working or trying to keep her five unruly children in line, Caroline enjoys watching ridiculous comedy, listening to gangster rap and talking to her rescue dog, a Chihuahua named Lola, with a terrible imitation of a Mexican accent.

Endnotes

[i] Source: http://www.tobaccoatlas.org/

[ii] Source: Global statistics on addictive behaviors: 2014 status report
http://onlinelibrary.wiley.com/doi/10.1111/add.12899/full

[iii]http://www.cdc.gov/tobacco/data_statistics/fact_sheets/health_effects/tobacco_related_mortality/

[iv]
http://www.surgeongeneral.gov/library/reports/50-years-of-progress/full-report.pdf

[v] http://www.webmd.com/erectile-dysfunction/news/20030307/smoking-can-lead-to-erectile-dysfunction

[vi] Jill Bolte Taylor: In the Garden of the Mind - Vision,

https://www.vision.org/visionmedia/interviews/jill-bolte-taylor-mind-and-brain/6(accessed August 23, 2016).

[vii] J.E. Prousky, 'Vitamin B-3 for nicotine addiction', Journal of Orthomolecular Medicine, Vol. 19(1) (2004), pp. 56–7

[viii] http://www.doctoryourself.com/hoffer_niacin.html

[ix] http://www.joanmathewslarson.com/HRC_2006/CorrectingChemistry.htm

[x] http://www.foodforthebrain.org/alzheimers-prevention/homocysteine-and-b-vitamins.aspx

[xi] http://healthland.time.com/2012/01/09/nicotine-gum-and-patch-dont-help-smokers-quit-long-term/

[xii] Ocular Compression - Canine Epilepsy Resources, http://www.canine-epilepsy.com/http://www.canine-epilepsy.com/Ocularcompression.html (accessed August 24, 2016).

[xiii] http://www.nobelprize.org/nobel_prizes/medicine/laureates/1937/szent-gyorgyi-lecture.pdf

[xiv] University of California - Los Angeles. (2007, June 22). Putting Feelings Into Words Produces Therapeutic Effects In The Brain. *ScienceDaily*.

Retrieved August 25, 2016 from
www.sciencedaily.com/releases/2007/06/07062209072
7.htmwww.sciencedaily.com/releases/2007/06/0706220
90727.htm

[xv] Efficacy of water preloading before main meals as strategy for weight loss in primary care patients with obesity
http://onlinelibrary.wiley.com/doi/10.1002/oby.21167/a bstracthttp://onlinelibrary.wiley.com/doi/10.1002/oby.2 1167/abstract

[xvi] Weight Loss and Water Consumption Appear to Be Linked. http://time.com/4403276/drink-water-hydration-weight-loss/http://time.com/4403276/drink-water-hydration-weight-loss/

[xvii] Alloxan in refined flour: A Diabetic concern 1 Shakila Banu.M, Sasikala.P
http://ijair.jctjournals.com/sept2012/t12930.pdfhttp://ija ir.jctjournals.com/sept2012/t12930.pdf

[xviii] http://non-gmoreport.com/articles/grim-reaper-many-food-crops-sprayed-with-weed-killer-before-harvest/ http://non-gmoreport.com/articles/grim-reaper-many-food-crops-sprayed-with-weed-killer-before-harvest/

[xix] http://www.ecowatch.com/15-health-problems-linked-to-monsantos-roundup-1882002128.html http://www.ecowatch.com/15-health-problems-linked-to-monsantos-roundup-1882002128.html

xx

http://articles.mercola.com/sites/articles/archive/2013/0
6/09/monsanto-roundup-herbicide.aspx

xxi How Gut Bacteria Help Make Us Fat and Thin
http://www.scientificamerican.com/article/how-gut-
bacteria-help-make-us-fat-and-
thin/http://www.scientificamerican.com/article/how-
gut-bacteria-help-make-us-fat-and-thin/

xxii Changes in rate and pattern of caffeine
metabolism after cigarette abstinence.
http://www.ncbi.nlm.nih.gov/pubmed/3365914http://w
ww.ncbi.nlm.nih.gov/pubmed/3365914

Made in the USA
Middletown, DE
05 October 2017